Going to Church with Children

by Stan Stewart

with Pauline Stewart and Richard Green

Joint Board of Christian Education
Melbourne

Published by
THE JOINT BOARD OF CHRISTIAN EDUCATION
Second Floor, 10 Queen street, Melbourne 3000, Australia

GOING TO CHURCH WITH CHILDREN

© Stan Stewart, Pauline Stewart, Richard Green 1987

National Library of Australia
  Cataloguing-in-Publication entry.

Stewart, Stan, 1937- .
  Going to church with children.

  ISBN 0 85819 622 0.

  1. Children — Religious life. 2. Worship (Religious education).
  I. Stewart, Pauline. II. Green, Richard, 1948-
  III. Joint Board of Christian Education. IV. Title.

248.8'2

First printed 1987

Design: Jennifer Richardson
Typeset: JBCE
Printer: Brown Prior Anderson Pty Ltd, Burwood

JB87/1420

Contents

Dedication

**Dedicated to the courageous parents,
pastors, educators and concerned
Christians who, by their words and
their example, have encouraged us to
write this book.
And dedicated to the children who have
worshipped with us and who have
taught us so much about what it means
to worship God as his people.**

Thank you

There are some people to whom the Stewarts owe special
thanks. These are people who by their hospitality or the provision of facilities have made the writing of this book possible in
this year of 1986. We list them here as a way of showing our
appreciation.

In the United States: Dena Green and Eldine and Lyle McLaren
of Los Angeles; in Orlando, Florida, at First Presbyterian Church,
Candy Van Der Weide, Dr Tino Ballesteros and Wayne and
Angela Dear. In Perth, Australia: Jan Davis, Dorothy MacEwan,
Bill and Janice Guimelli, Elizabeth Gosling, Allan and Edith
Taylor, Richard and Mavis Cleaver. In Christchurch, New Zea-
land: Sally and Dick Tripp. And last but not least in Melbourne:
Mavis Grierson, staff person with the Joint Board of Christian
Education.

Introduction

At this point in time (mid 1986), there is a small but increasing number of people in mainstream congregations who want to have children with them in the regular worship services of their church. These people are usually a minority in their congregation, and quite often a much misunderstood minority. At the forefront of this group are parents, both couples and solo parents, and quite a few grandparents. Some pastors, educators and people on worship committees also share this concern. Over the last ten years, we have talked with many of these either through our workshops or in correspondence.

It has become obvious to us that many of these people who believe that children should be coming into worship are often unsure about how to begin. Some are also unsure about the feasibility of the idea. From our own experience and the experiences of others, we know that it is not an impossible dream. That is why we have written this book: to help parents, pastors and congregations with a most urgent task.

As we began to write, we found that we could not avoid writing an introduction on 'why' going to church with children is important; these explanations make up the first part of this book. In this section we have outlined some of the reasons why having children in worship is of great importance not only to the children, but also to the entire congregation. In these chapters we point out that for congregations and denominations which are declining in numbers and optimism, going to church with children is a foremost necessity.

The truth is we must welcome children into worship not just because they need to be there (which they most certainly do) but because without them we cannot properly hear the gospel. This is a path to renewal but it is a path which has been overlooked in recent years. We hope that this book with its introduction and practical suggestions will help readers to uncover for themselves this hidden path to joy and growth.

Preface

A how to do it book

Most of this book is devoted to providing practical help to people who wish to go with children to Sunday by Sunday worship. For a complete explanation of what going to church with children means see 'Some Tough Definitions' on page 7.

With an introduction on why do it

In the introduction and in some other sections of the book, there is a particular focus on problems that are currently facing mainstream churches. Readers who belong to other denominations may or may not be facing similar situations in their own church. However, our guess is that most readers will find value in at least skimming through these sections. The problems they address are so much of the spirit of this age that it is almost impossible to avoid being influenced by them in some degree.

So, mix and match!

This is not a book that has to be read from the beginning to the end. It is more like a manual to be dipped into wherever and whenever there is something that will help you with a particular need. We encourage you to use the contents page and go directly to the section that speaks to your need.

On the other hand, if the whole subject is intriguing to you — go to it. We will do our best to see that one chapter flows into the next in a way that will make it easy for you to follow.

Let the reader beware

This book does not contain a set of formulas to be followed to the letter. Life has taught us that no one has all the answers on anything, and particularly on this subject of going to church with children. There are many different ways to approach the topics we deal with in this book. All we can say is that the suggestions we make have worked for us and we have seen them work for others. However, we are well aware that a different approach may work better for you. Our main concern is to help our readers in their thinking about and working at the task of going to church with children.

Personalise your plan of action

Here is the way in which we think this book may help you. Read what we have to share. Think lovingly about the children you have in mind and the church into which you want to take them. Pray about it. Then do what seems right to you. Once you have begun, be ready to stick with the enterprise over the long haul. Be ready to make changes to your approach if things do not work out. Be prepared to compromise if the situation demands it. But whatever you do, do not lose heart. Going to church with children may be one of the most important things which you can do in the service of your Lord and for the increase of his kingdom.

A primer to get you started

We are confident that there is no problem so large that it prevents going to church with children on a weekly basis in every local church. This book contains clues as to how most of the problems can be dealt with in a positive and fellowship building way. Note that we do not say 'easily'. For although the answers to most problems related to going to church with children are simple, few of them are easy. Many of them require a great deal of love, patience and work. Nonetheless, none of the ideas is so difficult as to prevent the smallest or the largest church from worshipping with their children. That is if this is something they really want to do.

Some tough definitions

Just before you get started, consider some tough definitions.

Going to worship

When this book talks about 'going to church with children' it is talking about taking them to the regular worship service of their church. This needs to be clearly stated at the outset because in the recent past, going to a mainstream church with children has not meant taking them to worship. It has frequently meant taking them to Sunday school, Junior Church, nursery or some other form of children's activity *only,* or instead of, taking them to worship.

Regularly

Note carefully that the worship referred to is the 'regular worship' of the congregation. This book is about going to church with children every week.

For the whole time

Nor is this book about taking children to worship for the first ten or fifteen minutes of a worship service. It is about helping children to stay through the entire length of a normal worship service.

And not just on special occasions

This book is not primarily about going with children to special childrens services, special family services or special seasonal services. We are all for the inclusion of these festival-type services in the calendar of any church. However, the focus of this book is on going with children to the regular, predictable, Sunday by Sunday worship of the congregation.

Not one, quick giant stride — but many, slow, tiny steps

We could encourage parents and congregations to aspire to this lofty aim. However, we understand that the goal will not normally be achieved with one giant step. For many children and for many congregations, there will be many stages on the way. For instance, one of these stages may be having children come into worship for a few moments only of the worship service. If this is the case, so be it. However, let it be clearly understod that this is to be seen just as a temporary stage on the way, and not the end of the journey.

All of this will lead to some tough consequences.

A stirring of unease

Quite a few people in congregations that are used to worshipping without their children will react with unease to what lies behind the definitions set out above. Some will be incredulous; others alarmed; and others just plain angry.

The ruination of worship for the aged

'Our old people do not like to have children with them in worship.' This is the most commonly heard complaint in congregations that are contemplating or commencing having children in church. It is hardly ever said by the old people themselves but usually by middle-aged persons who have nominated themselves as spokespersons for the aged. Frequently, persons making these comments have not consulted the old people directly. Rather, they are passing on what they 'feel' or 'guess' the old people are thinking. Nonetheless, it is true that about one third of the people of senior years in any congregation have hearing problems. These people find it easier to listen to anything when children are not present.

Denying parents spiritual nurture

In many cases, the most active opposition to going to church with children are the children's parents. 'It is a waste of time going to church if I have to sit with my children.' 'It is just a constant battle of wills which leaves me exhausted and the people around me annoyed.' With these and similar comments some parents vehemently attack the idea. Particularly vulnerable are solo parents who often are greatly stressed by life and who have a desperate need for some personal refreshment in worship. Here is a selection of the kinds of reactions which are likely to follow any suggestion that the 'tough definitions' be implemented.

Creating all kinds of difficulties for the pastor

Most pastors who have been used to leading worship in 'adults only' congregations do not welcome the idea of bringing the children back into church. The presence of children in the worship service introduces a volatile mix which they feel will make it more difficult for them to lead and for the congregation to follow. They can no longer be sure that everything will go exactly as they have planned. They fear that their beautiful services will be interrupted by the unlovely and unexpected sounds or actions of the children.

And then there's take and double take

The most disconcerting thing about these attitudes is that often they will not be clearly expressed until the children begin to appear in the worship service. Even after the matter has been thoroughly discussed and agreed to in advance, there can still be nasty shocks in store for people who want to come to church with children. It is a fact that some people who agree in principle to the idea of welcoming children into worship change their minds when they encounter the idea in practice. Winning over a congregation to accept the presence of children in worship is a battle that has to be won many times, not just once.

Legitimate complaints to a most worthy aim

Behind all the complaints are matters of real substance that must be faced by those who would go with children to church. Older people have a right to hear the Word of God, parents have spiritual needs, solo parents *must* have nurture and support, pastors are required to lead worship in a decent and orderly way. However, going to church with children does not have to get in the way of the fulfilment of any of these needs. But there is only one way to ensure that this does not happen. Those who would introduce children into congregations that have previously been childless must proceed with great care, patience and have a genuine respect for the needs of all involved.

We set out the ideas in this book in the hope that they will be applied with a gentle and loving spirit. Only if they are applied in this way will the whole body of Christ be built up. Only then will congregations experience the joyfulness and meaningfulness of worshipping together as the family of Jesus.

A tough conclusion

Nonetheless, the rub still remains. Getting started going to church with children is never going to be easy. To move in this direction in congregations that have grown used to worshipping without children will create discomfort for those who try it. Possibly it will stir up complaints and opposition in the councils of the congregation. Some families may even threaten to leave the church.

Why try?

If this is the case, why would anyone want to try to do such a thing? The short answer is (a) because it is of utmost importance to the children's spiritual development and (b) it is critically important for the life of the congregation and particularly the quality of their worship and their openness to the guidance of God.

Many people who read this book will need no convincing on these points. These folk can skip the following introduction and jump straight into the 'how to do it' heart of this book. Others will need to think about it some more. For them the chapters in the following introductory section may be of particular importance.

Chapter 1
There's a lot at stake

Slip sliding away

Mainstream Protestant and Anglican (Episcopalian) Churches in Australia, New Zealand and the United States have been declining in numbers for some years. The decline has been most pronounced in Australia and New Zealand, while in the United States the decline has taken a more gradual curve. However, the consistent direction of membership statistics over the last few years has been down. When added together, the small annual declines total up to a sizeable portion of these denominations former membership strength.

What decline?

For a number of years, nothing much was said within the mainstream denominations about the decline. One reason for this could be the dominant position that these denominations have held in the three countries. They perceived themselves to be part of an unshakable order or establishment and the pillars of decent society. They seemed to feel that a few years of decline could do nothing to change this. They had the kind of naive self-confidence which comes to those who feel that there can be no possible opposition.

But the decline has not stopped and the number of shrinking congregations is becoming painfully obvious. Leaders in local congregations and whole denominations are acknowledging 'Our denomination is in decline. We have a problem'.

No shortage of explanations

Now the cat is out of the bag, many are confident that they know who let it out and how it can be put back in. These opinions present a number of different points of view on congregational life. However, on one thing they seem to be united. The decline is very much related to problems in adult or youth ministry and the rot can only be stopped by focusing in this area. Children and childrens ministry either past, present or future hardly rates a mention in most of the popular theories. Here are a few examples.

Right principles will fix it

Success oriented ministers are more interested in understanding the dynamics of growth than in thinking about the reasons for decline. In recent years a number of these have built large churches at an impressive rate. These successful pastors talk as though church growth is a matter of following the right principles. These principles almost all relate to aspects of ministry with adults, such as public relations, church management, the follow up of new people and stewardship.

Terrible teens and whimpy youth leaders

For years there have been complaints about wayward, modern youth and criticism of youth programs and youth leaders. The decline in the number of young adults in these churches has often been tagged as a problem which flowed from insipid youth programs and ineffective youth leaders. The inference being, that once we have good youth leaders with dynamic youth programs, our denomination will start to grow again.

We need the old time religion

During the years of decline there has been an upsurge of evangelism of a fundamentalist type. People with enthusiasm for this kind of ministry have a simple answer: they see the decline as related to a lack of 'sound preaching'. In their view what is most needed is for denominations to repent of 'modernist' ways and return to the 'old time religion' particularly in the conduct and content of worship. This view has placed renewed stress on revivalism and in some cases 'hell fire' preaching — which is very much aimed at adults.

Holy Spirit power

Throughout the church there has been an upsurge of interest in the ministry of the Holy Spirit. Some aspects of this has led to the flowering of the charismatic movement. People from within this movement tend to see all of their denomination's problems as the direct result of a de-emphasis on the person and the ministry of the Holy Spirit. From their point of view, the most necessary step for renewal and growth is the infilling of the Holy Spirit in adults and teens, in congregations and in whole denominations.

They all seem to be right!

Each of the points of view mentioned above can provide proof that their view is the right one. In every case these folk can point to churches of their persuasion which have had tremendous growth rates. Some of these 'growth' churches are to be found within mainstream denominations. Others belong to different denominations or to no denomination. With this kind of evidence to back them, each point of view is confident that it has the answer to reversing the decline. Each in its own way has been saying to the contemporary church 'You don't have to decline. If you do things our way, our churches and our (or your) denomination can grow again'.

However, there is a factor in the growth equation of all of these points of view that is almost always overlooked.

How does their garden grow?

The truth is that much of the growth rate of many of the 'success' churches (successful for any of the reasons given above) comes at the expense of other churches in their neighbourhood or in their area. Frequently they draw their new members from the membership of many other churches and from a wide spectrum of denominations. However, it is not unusual for the 'success' churches in the mainstream denominations to draw their so-called 'new people' from churches of their own denomination. So while in a particular denomination some congregations have grown into super big churches, the overall pattern of decline in the churches in their denomination in their area continued. This pattern can be seen in mainstream churches across Australia and New Zealand and in many areas of the USA.

There must be something more

All of these points of view have had their say and have been heard in the councils of congregations and denominations. But, at the time that we write this book, there are some people (and our perception is that their numbers are increasing) who find all

13

of these answers unsatisfying — or at least only partly satisfying.
They sense that something else has been going wrong within the
life of their church and their denomination that none of these
scenarios seem to address.

We, the authors of this book, are confident that this 'something
else' has to do with the way these churches have been attempting
to nurture their children.

Flawed ministry with children?

Along with many others, we believe that part of this decline is
the result of mistaken theory and incorrect practices in some key
areas of ministry with children. This combination has meant that
these denominations have been experiencing increasing difficulty
in passing on faith and a sense of denominational identity to the
children of their faithful (church attending) adults. To put it
plainly, one of the major reasons why these denominations are in
decline is because they have been unable to enthuse and influence
yesterday's children. The people who are missing today from
their churches are the children of yesterday.

Chapter 2
A case of missing identity

The church had a number of flourishing youth groups. Over a hundred young people, ranging in age from early teens to early twenties, met each week in classes and clubs. The youth groups were the pride and joy of their church. Only one small thing caused concern. Although large numbers of them would come to the 'special youth services' only very few of them came to regular worship.

There were seven of the young people who were always at one of the worship services each Sunday. They did not come together; they did not sit together; nor did they arrive in the company of their parents. They were just there in church, at one of the regular worship services, every Sunday. These seven were no holy club. They attended the same groups and went to the same Saturday night parties as the rest of the young people. In fact the only way they deviated from the pattern of their peers was their regular church attendance.

It was the custom in this church to have an annual morning youth service, with the young people leading worship for the whole congregation. The service was planned by a small group of young people and on this occasion the supervising minister deliberately chose the seven young people (five teens and two young adults) who came regularly to worship.

Usually the youth were free to lead the service on whatever theme they felt fit. However, the minister did ask one thing. 'At some point in the service, I want you to make some response to this question: "Why is it that you seven are to found in church every Sunday and the rest of your friends are not?" ' After posing the question, the minister left the group alone to work out their response as seemed right to them.

The service reflected the group's enthusiasm and maturity. Prior to the sermon they assigned a two minute spot in which to respond to the minister's question. Here is the thrust of what their spokesperson said. 'We have had some difficulty in answering this question. When we started looking for what was different about us we could find hardly anything. We have the same interest and likes as our church friends. Nonetheless, the more we thought about it, the more obvious it became that we were different. Each of us confessed to having a deep, inner compulsion to go to church each Sunday. This was so pronounced that if a Sunday passed without us attending worship, we had the feeling that we had missed out on something. So we identified this as the major difference we had with our friends. Quite clearly, they had no such feeling or inner urging.

'We examined ourselves to try and understand why this feeling was in us. We shared stories of our Christian experience and our Christian growth. These varied a great deal. However, in one point we were all the same. All seven of us had been taken by our parents to worship every Sunday. From our babyhood onwards, we attended worship every Sunday. We can only presume that it is this common pattern which has planted in us the desire to come to worship week by week. It must have been this practice which has established in us the conviction that being in worship each Sunday is an important part of our lives.'

Whether children of church attending families grow up to be active members of that same church or denomination or not has a great deal to do with their sense of identity. A sense of identity is part of my individual background perception of who I am, and to whom I belong. It may not be an obvious thing either to the person concerned or to others. Nonetheless, this sense of identity will play an important part in deciding the person's preferences, loyalties and commitments.

We are convinced that in recent years, mainstream denominations have overlooked the importance of forming of a sense of church identity in children, especially young children. These denominations have worked hard at teaching their children lots of general information about the faith. They have not been effective in helping them to feel deeply that they belong to a particular church family and a particular denomination. This need not have been the case in the past and it certainly need not continue to be so in the future. Observation of how others form a sense of church identity show how this situation can be changed. Of the two major approaches the second will appeal most to mainstream churches and it leads directly to 'Going to church with children'.

Doing it late

All the growing, notably successful, congregations work hard to engender a strong sense of congregational identity, and in some cases denominational identity. In many and various ways, growing churches impress their members with a sense of their 'specialness'. They constantly remind old and new members that they belong to a 'special' church. Revivalist churches may refer to themselves as 'especially blessed' while more liberal congregations may simply say 'ours is no ordinary church' or 'this is a great church'. The claim to 'specialness' may be based on any number of things from a high level of mission-giving to enlightened preaching. However, what is important in all of them is that through language and through symbol they re-enforce within their members the notion that 'this church is on the ball, on the move. Ours is a special church and it's great to belong to it'. And 'because you belong to us, you are special'.

In this atmosphere, even newcomers are quickly caught up in this 'our church is special' feeling. In a surprisingly short space of time, the new congregation becomes 'my church' and through belonging to it the person finds meaning and excitement. The self proclaimed 'great church' gives to new and old members alike the feeling that 'I am on the winning side'. It becomes for them a valued element of self identity.

This positive feeling of identity is shot through some whole denominations, especially those who are aggressively evangelistic. Not surprisingly these denominations have experienced strong growth in recent years.

Doing it early

However, there is another way of passing on strong feelings of denominational identity. This method works quietly and unobtrusively. It can work as effectively in small churches as in large ones. Nor does it require that the congregation be constantly proclaiming its specialness. In fact as we mention below its effectiveness is not even impaired by internal controversies which bring sourness to individual congregations or even whole denominations.

This method sees early childhood as the time to imprint this sense of denominational identity. One of the major tools it uses is 'going to church with children'. Parents are urged to make weekly attendance at worship a regular occurrence for their babies and small children. Behind this method is the understanding that if we expose young children to the rhythms of our worship and the sights and sounds of our assembly then it will become part of them. In answer to the question 'Who am I?', the unconscious mind will reply amongst other things 'You are a church going person'.

A good example of this approach can be seen in the Roman Catholic Church. Centuries ago, the founder of the Jesuits, Ignatius Loyola said 'Give me a child until he is seven and he will be a Catholic for the rest of his life'. This slogan continues to be a guiding principle for that denomination. Despite the inner tensions which the Catholic Church has experienced in recent years, the work of imprinting their children with their Roman Catholicness continues without any decline in effort.

Denominations which consistently work at this early implanting of a sense of denominational identity have not experienced the spectacular growth of the revival churches and the totally positive, evangelical denominations. However, nor have they experienced anything like the extent of decline which has troubled the mainstream churches. It seems that people who at an early age come to feel that they belong to this or that denomination are likely to be loyal to it throughout their lives. This is so even when in later life they disagree with the edicts of their church — which has been the case with many Catholics in recent years. Such is the indelibleness of the stamp of identity.

Doing it never

The first approach does not fit easily into the ethos of most mainstream churches. Most of the leaders of their congregations have little taste for proclaiming their church as 'a great church'. In an ecumenical age, perhaps this is the result of a responsible and sincere approach to Christian missions. It could also be the result of a loss of enthusiasm or nerve.

These same churches have shown little inclination to work at implanting in their small children a sense of church or denominational identity. Their major commitment with persons in this age group seems to have been to supply them with a reasonably hygienic nursery with reasonably adequate staff. For the first four years of life, most of their children experience the church as a nursery. Sometimes the nursery has had a deliberately cultivated Christian atmosphere, sometimes it has not. Whatever the case, the bottom line is that the child experiences it as yet another nursery to grow out of and not as an awesome fellowship to grow up into.

The end result of this is that a person can grow up in a congregation without ever feeling any strong attachment to that church let alone the denomination. People who have come through this kind of church are likely to drift away from the church altogether or are prone to wander into other denominations.

Looking for something to believe in and someone to belong to

Here is what we perceive to be happening. Much of the growth in other denominations and non denominational churches is coming from the gathering in of young adults who as children and youth attended the mainstream churches. These young adults have been exposed to and educated by programs within their originating churches. These have aroused in them an interest in faith and the church. But, the totality of their experience in their original church never developed in them any sense of belonging or of love for their church.

As children many of them seldom experienced anything more than a Sunday school class. The idea that they belonged to a church made up of all ages and which was there for them for all of the ages of their life never dawned upon them. Only infrequently were they welcomed into the worship assemblies of their church. And then frequently they were bundled out of the services at the earliest possible opportunity. A sense that they were members of an all age fellowship of believers *(koinonia)* never had a chance to impact them at any depth. They lack any deep sense of a church homeplace. They do not have within their subconscious memories, echoes of sounds and rhythms of the worship of a people to which they belonged...

It is people who have travelled this route through the mainstream churches who are being won into the revival churches. For them the experience of worship and belonging to a church family is quite new. They do not see this as a betrayal of their old denomination, because they felt that they never belonged to it in any meaningful way.

A Divine withering?

Some people will see this as a good thing. In their minds the mainstream denominations have lost their vigour and vision. His *shekinah* (glory) is now to be found hovering over other churches and other denominations. The authors of this book, whilst not denying the energetic ministry of the revival churches, do not agree that God's Spirit has left the mainstream churches.

We do not believe that the decline of the mainstream denominations is part of God's will or plan. On the contrary we sense that God is calling these churches to 'gird up their loins' for future ministry and mission. However, we also believe that whether or not they will have the people to fulfil the work that God has placed before them will depend in part on what they do now about 'going to church with children'.

Babies in worship and adults in church

For any church, and particularly the mainstream churches, the best time to implant a durable sense of identity is in early childhood. To achieve this end, the most powerful influence they have is their worship services. It is through regular exposure to and participation in the worship services of their congregation that children (including small children and babies) are most likely to feel (not think) that this experience in this place is an important part of their lives. That is why going to church with children is so important for today's declining churches. It is not an answer to all of their problems, but it is an important first step towards stopping the rot.

Parents who want their children to grow up to be church attending adults should make going to church with their children a top priority. The leaders of their congregation, particularly leaders in mainstream denominations, should do all that they can to encourage this pattern. Congregations should welcome the children and be prepared to work at the task of developing in the children patterns of behaviour that are appropriate to the worship setting. These actions will have a positive effect on the vitality of today's congregations and the viability of tomorrow's.

P.S. · But don't misunderstand us

What we are saying is prone to misunderstanding. We are not suggesting that imprinting a church or denominational identity either late or early is all that there is to becoming a Christian. The three of us who write this book are evangelical in outlook and believe that if faith is to take root it must be as the result of a personal opening of the life to Jesus as Lord. However, what we find to be undeniably true is that a sense of church or denominational identity helps prepare the ground in which personal faith can grow. It becomes an inner source of motivation which

prompts the person to seek after spiritual nurture and for a spiritual home.

Another point at which we are often misunderstood is that some folk seem to feel that we are suggesting that any kind of exposure to worship will create a positive feeling towards that church in the inner self. This is clearly not the case. The way in which some individuals have experienced the church at an early age has bred within them negative intuitions towards the church and the Christian faith. A reading of the rest of this book will reveal the kind of positive experiences of worship which we know will be good for the child. It is these kinds of experiences which will lay a grounding for personal faith and a personal commitment to the nurturing church.

Chapter 3
Gifts for young and old

The public relations officer of the Drug Squad had just delivered a lecture on the situation with drug abuse in the city of
Perth. The story he told was of a large number of teens and
children experimenting with addictive substances. His audi-
ence was clearly disturbed. The chairman invited questions.

'Why do our young people turn to drugs?' The questioner
went on to list some of the many sporting, recreational and
entertainment facilities the city provided. 'What more do they
need?' Grunts of approval could be heard from around the room.

The sergeant moved to the microphone. 'It is often said that
the reason teenagers take drugs is because they are bored. We
agree with this. Many young people seem to start on drugs as a
way of escaping from boredom. And as you have suggested in
the way you have put the question, many people think that
being bored is the result of living in a community that lacks
facilities for teenage sport, recreation and entertainment. Now
these things help combat boredom in teens, but they are by no
means a complete answer. The reason for this is that being bored
has less to do with what surrounds a teenager — beaches, skat-
ing rinks and the like — than what is inside the teenager's head
and heart. In other words, boredom is an inner problem and not
an outer one.'

For a moment he stood there stroking his chin. 'What I am
saying here is that the boredom or frustration that drives many
teens to try drugs is deeply rooted in them. It comes not from
their experience of life as teenagers, but it is planted in them in
their earliest years of life — in fact in their pre-school years.'

These days there seems to be an expectation about that
children need to be constantly turned on, by that I mean smiling, jumping up and down. Parents live in dread of their child
saying to them 'I'm bored'. So as a way of preventing this,
children are hustled from one stimulation to another — new

places, new shows, new toys. When we constantly do this we are training our children to be tired of anything and everything in a very short time. We give them the impression that happiness is to be found in a never ending supply of new things and new experiences.

The other side of this coin is that any form of bodily or mental discomfort or pain is to be avoided at all costs. So parents dose their young children pills and potions all of the time. The message here is 'that if you're feeling down take a pill'.

This life-view is bred into many of our children before their first day at school. It comes to sound something like this. 'Feeling good is my birth right. Feeling bored is wrong. And so whatever turns you on is OK'. As they move into the teen years, and for many it's earlier than this, they start experimenting with alcohol as a means to feeling good. As this becomes ordinary, they begin to think about chemicals. And it all makes a kind of sense to them. After all, if the purpose of life is to feel good and to stay feeling good, or stimulated, or high, then obviously chemicals are the answer.

But this whole philosophy is a dirty lie. This is not a way of living. It is a way of dying. However, if this idea is to be defeated, parents must change. Parents must help their small children to realise that life is not about being turned on all of the time. They must help their children to be at ease in times of inactivity and to be comfortable with silence. Children must learn early that some forms of pain are friendly warnings to be respected, and not deadly enemies to be subdued with pain killers. And somehow they must help their children to realise the personal resource of their imagination and their capacity for inner creativity and inner adventures. Once children have discovered these truths about life and about themselves, they begin to develop their own defenses. From this vantage point of inner strength, they are able to see there are better things to do in life than to chase after the allusions created by drugs.

Mischievous misconceptions

'The worship service is not suitable for children, especially small children. There is nothing in it for them. To take children into worship is simply unfair on the child. It will bore them to tears. Because they are bored, they will wriggle and complain and distract whomever is sitting near them. Taking children to worship can only be a negative experience. It will make worship a

waste of time for the parents and may well put the children off church for life.'

These sentiments are often expressed by church going parents who belong to mainstream denominations. It is because they believe these things that they support all kinds of programs (and sometimes any kind of program) to get the children out of the worship service. 'After all, it's best for them and it's best for us.'

This line of thinking is encouraged by a coalition of influences in our society. Here are a couple of the most visible of these.

The advertising industry — 'happiness is'

These highly skilled professionals are employed by commercial interests to sell products designed for use by children or for consumption by children. To create a market for their client's products, the advertising industry creates an image of the happy child. This definition of the happy child always exactly suits the needs of their client. Invariably the happy child is holding, wearing or eating their client's product. According to the advertisements, the happy child is a child who is always smiling broadly, laughing loudly and moving excitedly.

Children who observe these images, especially through the medium of television, are impressed and usually envious. Quite naturally they want to be boisterously happy like the TV children.

It is a short step for them to think that this is the only kind of happiness. Once this point of view is established, the child is firmly set on the path which is littered with times and events that will cause him/her to say 'I'm bored'.

Many parents are also influenced by the advertiser's definition of the happy child. They begin to want their child to measure up to the media image. They want to see their child smiling broadly, laughing loudly and moving excitedly. What is more, they are prone to think that any time the child is not acting in this way, he/she is unhappy. This happens even with parents who in their minds acknowledge that these images are created simply to sell a product. It becomes easier to go along with this pervasive notion than to be repeatedly saying to their child 'life is not like this'.

For parents who consciously or unconsciously take it seriously, the advertiser's portrayal of the happy child is particularly discouraging to going to church with their children. Attendance at worship requires from the child behaviour which is the exact opposite to the advertiser's definition. Instead of encouraging their children to laugh loudly and to move excitedly, parents who go with children to worship will be asking them to talk softly (if they have to talk at all) and move slowly and quietly (if they have to move at all). As for smiling broadly, although there is no reason why this should not happen, it is unlikely that the child who sits during worship will do much of this. It is more likely that the child's expression will range from an occasional scowl ('How long will it be now?') to a quiet smile directed to a friend sitting in another pew. Most of the time for most children the look on their faces will be serious or thoughtful.

So parents who feel that their children should be happy in a TV advertisement kind of way, all of the time (apart from school hours that is — 'They have to go to school whether they like it or not; it's important for their future') find that going to church with children is a counterproductive exercise. In forming this opinion they show that they have been misled as to the true nature of happiness. Also, they are revealing that they lack any understanding of the long term benefits which can flow to their children from being part of a worshipping community.

This high powered image of the happy child creates many other difficulties for those who would nurture children in the Christian faith. The message implicit in most advertising is that 'happiness comes with owning, eating or being entertained'. The advertisers deliberately work to develop in children an 'I want it' or 'I want more' reflex. In parents they endeavour to promote the proposition that all of their child's needs could be met through things or special experiences all of which are available at a price. Few notions could be further from the Christian view of life than these points of view. In fact if parents wish to reinforce in their children the principles Christ taught, then they must deliberately work to negate the advertiser's view of happiness.

Christian parents have the task of steering their children against the tide of the superficial activism and the materialism of our day. They need to establish in thought and in fact some different definitions of the happy children. These will not overlook the child's need for acting out in a joyful and excited way. But they will also include the place of quiet times and the need for moments of calm reflection. Included in them will be an acknowledgment that not all of life will be wildly exciting. These will help children to understand that life will hold for them many times when little is happening and time goes slowly. Such times will not be labeled as 'unhappy' but rather as times to be coped with and opportunities for the development of imagination and inner resources. And central in this definition will be the spirit of thankfulness and the willingness to share.

Surprising as it may seem to many Christian parents, one of the most effective tools to help them forge these images is the worship service of their church. Perhaps more than anything else, a good experience of this service can help children begin to appreciate that belonging to Jesus means you are different. It helps them sense that sometimes being quiet is very important. They feel the moods and rhythms of worship and note how different it is from anything else they ever experience. They feel the strength of being part of a community which is united in its love for Jesus.

At an early age, children who are regularly in worship begin to note that their family and their extended family at the church have a different set of values to those they see and feel through television and other media. As with the television images, these values are enshrined in some oft-repeated images. The way in which their whole congregation gives attention and respect to these images helps the children to put these in a place apart in their hearts and minds. This does not mean that they turn away from the television and advertising images. They will still probably see these as desirable and exciting. However they will not be the only definitions they have of what it means to live a good and happy life. They will have begun to feel that for my family and for me, following Jesus is the best thing and the first thing. In fact it is the most important thing of all.

The school and principles of education

Ideas which come from schools and education seem to add intellectual respectability to this idea that 'children and worship don't mix'. Educators talk about such things as a child's concentration span and the child's need for 'appropriate' learning experiences. Their insights are of the utmost importance in the fields for which they were intended — that is helping children to gain literacy and number skills. However, the educator's insights are not valid for all of life's experiences. For instance, it clearly would be ludicrous to apply their ideas of readiness and concentration span when taking children to family gatherings. 'At what age is a child ready to spend thirty minutes with an aged aunt whose mind wanders and who only talks about adult memories?' 'At what age is a child "ready" to spend two hours in a shopping centre?' Most of a child's early life experiences are of this kind. It is simply not appropriate to apply the educator's principles to these kinds of learning encounters.

This judgment of the worship service based on educational principles has led to practices which have institutionalised the view that the worship service is no place for children. In Great Britain, New Zealand and Australia, it has taken the form of Sunday schools which are conducted at the same time as church. In the United States it has led to the establishment of children's church and other programs which operate concurrently with worship. These practices place enormous stumbling blocks in the way of the faith development of children. They also degrade worship for adults by creating 'R Rated' or 'Adults Only' worship. All of these bad things happen because of the sloppy assumption that at its heart, worship is an educational event.

The worship services of the church are not primarily educational experiences. Certainly they are educational and some aspect of the worship service can have a deliberate teaching intent. But the purpose of the worship service is to praise God and to open the congregation to the mystery of his presence. This is not something that any particular age group understands or can ever fully understand. In the worship service, everyone — old and young, scholar and illiterate — acknowledge that 'I am but a scholar in thy school — and at best a slow learner'.

This being the case, it is surprising that so many Christian parents still behave as though the worship service is a class and the church building is a class room. When thought of in these terms, the worship service and the place of worship are obviously not suitable for children. But this is a mistake of the most basic kind.

We must help our parents to recognise that they should take their children to church not to learn as they learn in school, but to feel. The worship service is full of feelings that the child will not feel at any other time in the week. Feelings of welcome, of community, of occasion, or importance, of reverence and awe should all cluster around this event. And we must help our children to know that all of these have something to do with Jesus and the fact that he loves me. For the young child, a positive experience of these feelings will be character and value shaping and will have a great influence on life direction.

Chapter 4
Helping the children I
Creating the spiritual and psychological environment which will enable children to feel welcome and at home in worship.

Preparing children to feel comfortable in worship involves many things. Some of these things are practical. The majority of the how-to-do-it suggestions in the next three chapters are based on enlightened common sense.

Other aspects of this preparation process are of a spiritual and psychological nature. The suggestions which relate to these aspects are more subtle and can easily be overlooked. Nonetheless, they will exercise great power on the formation of the child's attitude to church attendance.

Children need to be needed

Children fear being left out. They feel a need to be included in important things and to be welcomed in important places. Added to this, most children feel a need to please and to help the adults who are significant to them. Going to church with a caring adult who believes that worship is a high and holy act can be one way in which all of these needs are catered for.

But, notice this will by no means happen automatically. It will not happen if going to worship is something which is pushed on the child by an adult who is insensitive to the child's needs. Nor will it happen if the adult only attends worship out of some sense of duty or obligation. The rule of thumb here is: 'It is unreasonable to expect that any child you bring to a worship service will be more enthused about the service than you are'.

In the practical section of this and the following chapter, tasks and acts in which children can participate are listed. However, it must never be forgotten that there is more to having a child participate in worship than simply having a child hold a book or join in a response. Real participation involves helping a child feel that he or she is a valued person in the gathering. In other words, a person of any age participates when he or she feels that their presence is 'needed'.

This message of welcome and respect can be transmitted to children in many different ways. Most of these ways are informal and unstructured. Almost always the foundation for this feeling has been laid in times beyond the hour of worship. It can only be passed on by adults who really do care about children and to whom going to church with children is important. It is most effectively passed on by persons (especially worship leaders) who realise that the congregation needs to have children with them when they gather to hear the gospel. Without this purposeful intention to 'welcome children into worship', other steps such as giving children hymnals will have little more than a superficial, cosmetic impact.

The opening story of this chapter illustrates how a child who lacked a supporting church family received this 'I am needed' message from an adult friend. Help of this kind from an adult other than a parent is also needed by many children of church-attending families. All children of solo parent families need some assistance of this kind.

'The people at the church need me'

It was a wet and chilly Sunday morning. The kind of morning when people are tempted not to go to church and Sunday school. Actually, the weather had not dampened my enthusiasm at all. However, it had provided my non-church attending parents with a good argument to persuade me not to go. Ever since we had moved into town, only one mile from the local church, I had been going to church and Sunday school alone. My sisters had long ago opted to stay home or go to other places. At eight years of age, I loved to go and even on this cold winter morning, I looked forward to being at church and Sunday school.

I had laid out my favourite Sunday clothes. As my mother was giving them a last minute freshen up, she had accidentally scorched my shirt. My family presumed that the combination of a wet cold morning and a scorched shirt would keep me at home that day. (I was always meticulous about my dress.) Although this setback hurt me sorely, it made me all the more determined to go.

'Why do you have to go?' my mother questioned.

'I have to go', I blurted out.

'Why do you have to go?' questioned a sceptical sister.

'Because the people at the church need me.'

My mother and sisters looked on incredulously. It was beyond their comprehension that the local Methodist Church with all its bustling life could need their eight year old family member.

Then it came to me. Suddenly I had the other reason why I had to go. 'This will surely convince them', I thought.

'If I don't go, Mr Markwell will miss me!' and with that, I placed my hands on my hips and closed the conversation.

Years later, my mother still tells me about the determined look I had on my face. Whatever it was, it worked. No further time was spent on trying to persuade me not to go to church. A sister's blouse was hurriedly ironed and I was on my way.

The recollection of this incident reminds me that even at an early age I had a deep sense of feeling part of the church. I felt that my presence mattered. At eight years of age, when I went to church, I did not go as a spectator. I went as a participant, a participant in the deepest meaning of the word.

I believe that now I understand in part at least how this feeling was nurtured within me.

It had to do with the little jobs I used to do around the church. Actually, I had no official duty. Helping stack the hymn books and tidying the papers on the pews were tasks I loved to do. No one had ever really invited me to do them and I hadn't sought anyone's permission or officially volunteered. No one made a fuss over me either. I liked to help and so I did. My memories are of adults and other children sharing in this. Still, deep down I had the feeling that keeping the church working and preparing it for worship was in part my responsibility.

It has a great deal to do with Mr Markwell. At the time of the story, he had long since retired. I thought of him as my special friend. Certainly, he always looked for me and he never missed shaking my hand and asking about my life and family. But, there was more to it than that.

Mr Markwell and I were friends. At eight years, I was quite confident of that. I truly did believe that he would miss me. He made me feel special and I sensed that he thought of me as a friend and not just a kid. Certainly he remembered things about me — my interests, my family and always in his face I felt his care. We often didn't sit in the same pew but he was always there. So I felt that I should be always there.

Our relationship went back a number of years. Mr Markwell had visited our humble home (it was little more than a shack) when we lived in the bush some miles from town. He invited our family to come to church. My parents declined but said that the children could go if they wanted to. At that time we all jumped at the opportunity. We had ulterior motives. Going to Sunday school and church would provide us with an outing. The main feature of this outing would be a ride in Mr Markwell's new car. As we were without a car, this ride was a novelty which we greatly prized. When we moved to town, we were within walking distance of the church. It was at this point that my sisters grew tired of going to church. Not me, though, and I could tell that Mr Markwell was very pleased about this.

These are the kind of experiences which make an eight year old proclaim 'the people at church need me'. I now suspect that behind Mr Markwell's many acts of friendship was a practice of daily prayer for me. Small wonder I said 'Mr Markwell will miss me'.

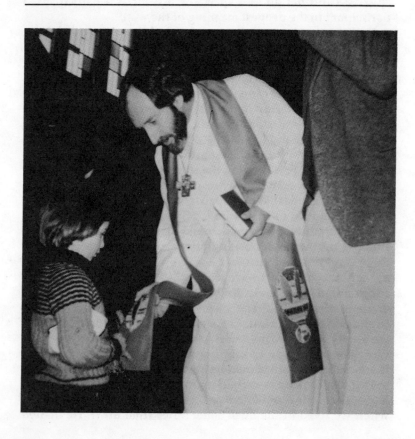

Does your congregation 'need' your children?

Here are two questions to think about and some suggestions worth trying.

The need to be needed

In your congregation are there practical things that children can do in relation to the worship service?

Note that these things need not be in the service. As with my experience, they may be tasks to be performed after the service. Experience has taught us that not every child has to be employed every Sunday. However, in and around every worship service, there has to be a range of tasks which children can do — even if each Sunday only a few children are involved on a roster basis. Many of these tasks need not be structured. They simply evolve as adults allow children to stand beside them and have a part in what they are doing — that is how I got started. These tasks, be they formally organised or informally evolved, are signs and symbols to children of all ages. They say that when the congregation gathers to worship God, children can help with some aspect of this high and holy occasion. It is on the basis of involvement of this kind that children come to feel 'my church needs me'.

In the second part of this chapter, there are examples of the wide range of things children are doing in some churches.

The feeling that I will be missed

Are there adults in your congregation who are developing friendships with individual children? Are you?

Here we are not just talking about Sunday school teachers. Children expect that their Sunday school teachers will miss them. It is their job to miss them. In the preceding story, the child was really impressed by the fact that an adult who never taught her, missed her. Her adult friend was a friend because he liked her and not because he taught her.

This is everyone's task. It even applies to the parents of young children. Just as their children will need to receive these vibes from other adults, so they must give these same signals to other people's children. Even parents who feel that they are not being very effective with their own children should work at this task. Frequently they will find that other people's children will respond to their offer of friendship with enthusiasm.

Watch the children in your church, in your family, and see if this kind of relationship is being offered to them. If not, take steps to encourage adults (especially older adults like Mr Markwell) to see this as an important ministry. Give a lead by working on such relationships yourself.

When talking about the need for adults to make friends with individual children, avoid making it sound too onerous. In fact it can be as easy as this:

> Watch for a particular child each Sunday and shoot him/her a friendly smile whenever possible.
>
> Learn this child's name and make sure he/she knows yours.
>
> Try to talk (even if only briefly) with this child at least once each Sunday. Note: talking with includes listening too.
>
> Express pleasure in the child's church attendance and encourage him/her in Christian things whenever the opportunity presents itself.

In many cases, the relationship will quite naturally extend to extra curricular, out of church activities. Where this happens, it will further strengthen the influence of the relationship. But even relationships which are limied to 'at church contact only' can plant in a child the notion 'my church friend will miss me if I do not attend'.

An obligation or an encouragement?

Some may see the nourishing of this 'I will be missed' feeling as placing upon a child an unnecessary obligation. Certainly it does place on the child a sense of responsibility. However, more importantly it says to the child 'I belong to something where my presence counts'. And by no means is this some ordinary 'something'. This 'something' includes all ages — probably the only all age gathering the child ever attends, and its gathering is for the most serious and holy purpose. Being a valued participant in this gathering is an experience of belonging to community. For today's children it is a unique experience of immense value for the foundation of the self image and life directions.

Here is a smorgasbord of suggestions for 'at home' preparation to help children in a practical way

Preparing small children at home

'Sunday morning is the grumpiest morning of the week. This is true for many Christian families. People tend to sleep late and then there is a frantic search for good shoes and "church" clothes.

There is a lack of routine and a maximum of confusion. This situation is ideal for creating frayed tempers and negative feelings. These negative vibrations accompany the family to church. Once there, adults may be able to shrug them off, but our children find it more difficult. But, Sunday morning need not be like that.'

These excellent suggestions for preparing small children for the Sunday worship service were prepared by Jill Firth whose husband, Len, is the minister of an Anglican parish in suburban Perth. It is a congregation which is experiencing an explosion in the numbers of small children. Jill and Len are parents of three of these.

Jill's suggestions on preparing children at home have been thoroughly field tested. It was a feeling of personal necessity which spurred her on to develop them. As her confidence in the procedures increased, Jill began to share them with families with similar needs in her parish. Families who followed these procedures found that they also worked for their children. Their small children started to look forward to going to worship. Instead of being forever restive, the children were comfortable in the service even when things were not particularly interesting to them.

These approaches have worked well with pre-schoolers through to late primary age children (eleven years).

Initially, Jill put her thoughts into print as a contribution to their parish magazine. Later they were given much wider circulation when they were re-published in *A People To Belong To* magazine.

During the week

1. Find time for yourself
Make time during the week to be alone with God, to pray, listen and read — then you will not be so resentful if the children are distracting on Sundays.

2. Share your faith
Pray with and for your child — use loving touch, a cuddle, hold hands, or laying on of hands.

Sing hymns and church songs with and for your child — this is fun, and it's a good way to worship. The child also learns the words.

Talk about your faith — how God is helping you right now. Tell your child about prayers for which you are awaiting answers, things you like about church, things you find hard about the Christian way.

3. Talk about worship

Children love to know 'why?', 'what does it mean?' Tell them about the parts of the worship service. Explain why we have prayers, songs, readings, sermon, offertory, greeting of peace, confession, communion, blessing, etc. Do it little by little — you can make a game of it. Do not presume that your small child is too young to understand. As long as the child is interested, something positive is going on.

4. Practise the responses

Teach your pre-schooler one response each week. For example Anglican families could practise — (parent) Peace be with you: (child) and also with you; (parent) This is the Word of the Lord: (child) Thanks be to God; and other responses used regularly in the worship. Non Anglicans will have similar things they can teach their children. Think about your worship and find something that is regularly repeated: an introit, the doxology, a benediction and teach this to your child.

Remember, children work on a feeling level. What we are doing in all of the above is teaching the child to master the rhythm of worship and so feel at home in the service. The deeper meanings of these things will come as they worship through the years.

On Saturdays

1. With your child, lay out: clothes for Sunday; their offering; choose a flower for altar bowl; special church books, Bible, activities, etc.

2. Talk about your own feelings about going to worship on the next day.

3. Agree on what the child can do if he or she gets restless, e.g. change seats, spend time with another adult, occupy themselves with a suitable activity, have 'time out'.

4. With a school-aged child, you can read through the Bible readings for Sunday.

Sundays

1. Choose a seat where children can see and hear and also have access to back of church, an aisle, toilets, etc.

2. Remember — children learn most from your attitude of caring and acceptance, and your willingness to help them worship.

3. We pause in the service before prayers of thanksgiving, intercession, confession — the children draw a picture of their prayer

need, the adults write their concern. Then we offer prayers to God verbally, either in small group prayers or someone leads the prayers. It seem to help everyone to focus much better.

Helping children feel comfortable in worship

It's all a matter of nurturing CALM SHEEP.

We (Stan and Pauline Stewart) use this acrostic as a memory aid for parents and grandparents. It is a summary of some of the key elements in this process of preparation. It is particularly appropriate for use between the ages of one year and six years, though some elements in it apply to all children.

CALM — things to do at home

C stands for 'calm them at home'

Some parents seem to expect their children to be calm and quiet in church when they are never that way at home. Parents (parent/grandparent) must build into the rhythm of their home times of quiet and calm.

This has two aspects to it.

1. Their children should see them in attitudes of quiet (television off, hi-fi off) reflection — especially, though not only, in relation to some devotional act, e.g. Bible study, prayer.

2. They must encourage their children to enter into and enjoy times of quiet. Some of these should be of a devotional nature but others can be focused around some aspect of nature and the appreciation of peaceful music. (See also 'Music' later in this section.)

This at home training will prepare in the child the capacity to enter into the reflective mood of the worship service. In other words, when in a church service the parent says to the child 'Now it is time to be quiet', they are not speaking in a vacuum of meaning. The concept of 'comfortable quiet', 'valued quiet' has already begun to take root in the child's life.

A stands for 'anticipate'

Sunday morning can be the grumpiest morning of the week even in many Christian households. Some of this grumpiness relates to the effort of going to church when non-church neighbours are sleeping or relaxing. Much of it is due to sheer disorganisation and can be alleviated by anticipation.

One aspect of this involves preparing clothes the night before. The simple act of laying out special clothes for a special day can help children to think positively about going to church.

The second aspect is to anticipate what can go wrong in the service. With babies this will involve preparing suitable wipe cloths, snacks, etc. With small and older children, it should involve talking through with them how they will cope with such things as restlessness and the slow passing of time. This may lead to the packing of a 'Church Bag' of appropriate activities or deciding in advance which adult friend the child could quietly visit with during the service. It should also involve discussing what action would be 'fair' to take in the event of the child becoming noisy to the point of distraction. Most children will respond with sensible suggestions to questions of this kind. Once the action is agreed about in advance, it strengthens the parent's hand in the worship setting.

Another side to this is to share with the child the things that they can look forward to. There may be a special music contribution or a celebration of one of the church seasons. By informing the children of this, there is the basis for excited anticipation of good things.

L stands for 'love worship'

This sounds obvious but it is often overlooked. Children quite often hear their parents grumble about church people and the demands, disappointments and stresses of church life. They may not hear much from their parents about the importance of worship for them and the value they place upon it. Christian parents (and grandparents) must find many different ways of telling their children about their love for Jesus and of how much they love to worship him. This communication must be in deeds as well as words — but the words are important.

Story telling is the most powerful medium here. For parents and grandparents, there are many stories tucked away in memory lane which illustrate the importance that going to worship has had to them. They should tell their children these stories of special places, occasions and important people associated with the churches of their childhood. Children have an avid interest in their family's history and it is important that parents and grandparents make time to tell them of the Christian dimension of their own life story.

M stands for 'music'

A large proportion of the music children hear in childhood is remembered for a lifetime. To an important extent, the music that children hear will often influence their adult taste in music. Music can also be used to predispose children towards feeling at home when their congregation gathers for worship. However, not all music on a Christian theme will do this. The children must hear hymns sung in a somewhat similar way that their congregation sing them.

Quite a proportion of Christian music on tape and records sounds just like secular music of the 'beautiful music' variety. Even Christian songs recorded especially for children sound just like secular nursery songs. Children can be surrounded with this kind of music from birth and still make no connections between this music and the music of the worship service.

The singing and the playing of hymns should be part of the background music of family life for the child. Babies find the sounds of congregational singing to be very soothing. Small children will come to love the hymns of their church as readily as they will love any other form of music. Once this is familiar to the child, the sounds of their congregation at worship will be a welcome sound in their ears. See the story of 'Walker and the Red Player' later in this chapter.

SHEEP — things to be done at church

S stands for 'sit with care'

Choosing where to sit is a key decision for successfully going to church with children.

Some seating situations invite disaster. For instance, to sit with a baby or toddler in the middle of a crowded pew is likely to lead to discomfort and disruption for many — not the least of whom will be the child and his/her adult companions. To locate lots of children in one pew or in one part of the church will almost always lead to outbursts of disturbing behaviour.

A seating position which is chosen with care can keep disaster at bay. It can also minimise the occasions for irritation and provocation for children and their adult companions. For instance, persons with babies and toddlers should sit in positions from which they can move to exits with the minimum of fuss. In most churches, the aisle end of a pew is the best position for this. When children are in a restless phase, the aisle end seats of the back pews may be the only pews to suit the children's needs.

Another factor which has bearing on the choice of a seat is what the child will see. Children should be located in positions where they are able to see something of interest to them. Many babies are fascinated by patterns of light. These children enjoy looking at stained glass windows and patterns of light and shade. Older children often prefer a good view of the congregation and the worship leaders.

Children who have adult friends they are allowed to visit during the worship service should be seated so as to allow easy access to them.

Children who need to sit near other children should be adequately separated from them by adults or at least located close to caring adult supervisors.

H stands for 'help by providing helpers'

Children and parents will cope better with going to church together if they have some extra help. This can best be provided by individuals who have a caring relationship with a particular child and his/her parents or parent. In most cases this help will be available as the result of prior arrangements. Sometimes it will arise spontaneously in a worship service as the result of the sensitivity of a caring adult.

However it happens, the helper will be available to the child during the service. This means that the child can quietly move to their adult friend at some appropriate part of the service, e.g. during the singing of a hymn. The adult helper will have made some provisions for this visit. These will include a space in which the child can sit beside them, a readiness to extend to the child some words of friendship and an embrace and most probably some object of interest (a small soft toy) and/or activity (a small pad and pencil) and perhaps something chewable. Helpers should consult parents as to what they would like them to provide for their children (for instance, some parents are anti-candy) and then respect their wishes.

On many occasions, children will move to their helpers according to their own whim. At other times, a parent will suggest the move. On a few occasions, the helper will come to the child and whisper an invitation to the child to come and sit with them. However it happens, small children rarely sit with their helpers for more than a few minutes. After a short visit, they will usually return to their parents or parent. Nonetheless, even a short visit can make an immense difference to the child's disposition. It is as though it discharges a build up of static energy that threatens to become explosive.

There should be a couple of rules governing these movements. One would be that the child must make their visits on tip toes. Another should be guidelines as to when such moves are allowable. For instance, it is not appropriate to move around during a prayer, but it is fine to move during the singing of a hymn or the sermon. In addition to these, some parents may want to limit the number of movements in the duration of the service, for example only two visits per service.

Helpers who assist parents with babies have a position of particular trust. They must be able to take the child when he/she is distressed or distracting and effectively give comfort and care. And they must be able to do this in such a way that the parents are at ease with their intervention.

Help of this kind with small children and babies is essential for solo parent families. Without it, many of them will find little value in attending worship with their children. When it is provided, it allows them to enter into the service in a way that is often not possible if they must spend the time struggling to control their child(ren).

Help of this kind is wonderful for children and especially the children of solo families. It is a wonderful embodiment of the family nature of the church.

For all children and parents who receive this kind of help, it puts flesh on the bones of the idea of belonging to the people of God. It is an affirmative, first hand experience of what it me ns to belong to the household of faith.

These helping relationships can only work on the basis of friendship and trust between the child and the helper and usually between the helper and the parents or parent. If this is not present, then children will object and the arrangement will be of little value. This means that most helper relationships will need to be deliberately nourished beyond the time of the worship service itself.

E stands for 'exit when necessary'

Some parents seem to feel that children should be in the worship service at all times, under all circumstances. We do not hold this opinion. There will come times in the life of almost every child when he/she will have to be taken out of the service. These will be such times as:

When the child is very distressed for any reason.

When the child has a very savage attack of ants in his/her pants.

When the child resists behaving in a manner appropriate to the worship service — that is, insists on running about and/or calling out loudly.

When the child has set up a distracting relationship or pattern of play with another child.

When a child needs to go to the toilet or is in danger of dying (?) of thirst.

In these circumstances, children should be removed from worship in a way that is respectful to the dignity of the service and the dignity of the child. In most cases, this dignified movement will be aided by moving earlier rather than late. The spectacle of a child being carried kicking and screaming from church is not helpful to anyone. Also, if the child is taken out before things have deteriorated too far, then the actions and negotiations mentioned in 'anticipate' above are more likely to be successful.

Parents and helpers should develop a sense of judgment as to when a child should be taken out. When a child can be satisfactorily hushed within the context of worship, it is better to do this. Sometimes children are taken out when their behaviour is well within acceptable limits or when a simple word or action would quieten them. We know of occasions when a parent — in this case it was a father craving for a smoke — purposely provoked his child to provide him with an excuse for leaving the service. This is naughty!

This exiting of the disruptive child is important for everyone.

It is important for the congregation and the worship leader. They have a right to be able to apply themselves to the worship of God without undue distraction.

It is important for the parent. It provides them with a prime opportunity to help their children discern that the worship occasion is 'different' from any other gathering. This educational opportunity is there even when the child is taken out by someone other than the parent.

It is *most* important for the child. It is one of the most effective ways to teach the child about the specialness of the occasion of congregational worship. It helps him/her to realise that this gathering is like none other and that it requires of everyone a particular kind of response.

If the child is never taken out and allowed to behave, however the mood takes him/her, then the child will be slow to grasp this distinction. As the result of this, the child's visit to the worship service will lack any heightened awareness of its importance. It will be ranked on the same level as a visit to the supermarket or an activity time in the kindergarten playground.

E stands for 'enter when the cause of the child's distress is resolved'

Parents and helpers must realise that taking the child out is only step one. Bring the child back into the worship service when he/she is calm again is step two. In fact, if the child is allowed or encouraged to stay out for the remainder of the service, then this will render the whole exercise counter-productive. In time, this behaviour tells the child messages like these: 'If I act in a certain way, I can be taken from the service and spend the rest of the time playing or walking and talking with my parent/helper'. The child will perceive this as some benefit they have gained and once they are aware as to how this can be obtained, they will seek to benefit as often as possible.

Rather the strategy must be this.

Meet the child's needs, whether they be physical or emotional or both.

Assure the child of your continuing affection and goodwill. This is especially important if the child has been sick or made some kind of scene.

Explain to the child that both of you must now go back into the worship service — stress the importance of the occasion to you and how much you and the child will be missed if you do not return.

Enter the worship service as quietly and as unobtrusively as possible.

With some children on some days, this exit/enter procedure must be used on a number of occasions during the one service. This is fine. If proceeded with kindly and with sensitivity to the child, he/she will soon get the message and realise that when they are feeling well, there is no other option to being in worship.

The quietening and soothing of babies frequently requires that they be held and gently rocked. Often the best way to do this is while their parent or adult helper walks the floor with them. Many churches have an area at the back of the pews where it is possible to walk without causing disturbance to the congregation. In cases where this is possible, the entry of a baby back into the service may have two stages — stage one being the soothing of the child outside the worship sanctuary and stage two a further settling of the child (perhaps to sleep) as the parent or helper walks quietly across the back of the pews inside the sanctuary.

P stands for 'persevere'

Anyone who wants to can make a success of going to church with children. What is meant here by 'success' is establishing the capacity in child and parent to find in going to church together a certain amount of comfort and meaning. However, the parent or the adult helper must 'want to' with a fair amount of resolve. This resolve will be tested in many ways as success will come only to those who persevere.

The parent and/or helper must persevere in the face of the following:

The child's complaints.

These most usually take these lines: 'Why do I have to go to worship when most of my friends do not?' or 'Why do I have to stay in worship while my friends go out to Sunday school or creche?' and 'This is boring'. Every child will try this approach. There is material in the introductory chapters which can help with this.

The suggestions of persons who lead the Sunday school (that is when it is organised at the same time as worship) and the creche or nursery staff.

These will run something like this: 'We have an activity especially for children, you know'. 'May I take your child to creche?' 'It's not really fair on children to stay through the whole service'. 'Are you unsatisfied with the standard of our creche or Sunday school?' 'H'mm, adults in our service like to worship in peace'. 'The service is not relevant to the needs of children. Our children's program is and the children enjoy it'.

The comments of other parents who think that persons who want to go to church with children are odd or nuts.

They are inclined to say things like: 'I know that it's much too boring for my children'. 'I feel that forcing them to go when they are young will only turn them away when they are older'. 'It's not really fair on the children'. 'Parents who force their children to attend church must be trying to make a good impression'.

The opposition of pastors and worship leaders to the idea of children in worship.

Thankfully this is not the most common problem, but when it does occur it is difficult to handle. This opposition is seldom expressed in a direct fashion. It is more often than not felt in pointed asides, inuendos and glares.

Persevering in the face of all this requires a deal of internal fortitude. But for parents who want their children to grow up to be church attending Christians, it must be done. There are no short cuts. There are no substitutes. See the 'emergency plan' at the conclusion of this book. For your children's future grounding in the faith and your own survival, you may need to activate it.

Walker and the Red Player

In October 1985 a baby son was born into our family. We named him Walker and from his earliest days I thought about preparing in him a love for Jesus and his church. From his first Sunday, Walker was in worship. But it seemed to me that taking him to worship each week was not enough. I wanted him to be in a positive frame of mind about worship when he arrived there. As I thought about this, I began to remember things that I had read about babies and music.

I had read several articles about babies and classical music. In these, parents who want their children to grow up to love classical music are advised to play this type of music to their babies. It appears that babies who grow accustomed to the strains (not too loud) of classical music wafting around them grow into children with a predilection for this kind of music.

My principal concern was that Walker should grow up to love the worship of Jesus in his church. Now a large part of the expression of that worship is a musical expression, particularly in the singing of hymns by the congregation. It then dawned on me that I should play our baby the hymns of the church.

We have in the house a bright red portable cassette player. This was obviously the ideal vehicle through which the music could be played. At first I puzzled over the recordings I should use. I ruled out Christian pop music on the grounds that this did not sound the least bit like the singing of our congregation. For the same reason, hymns sung by philharmonia choirs backed with symphony orchestras were also unsuitable.

Then I remembered that we had a set of cassettes which were nothing but hymns. This set was given to us by our good friends from the Reorganised Latter Day Saints when a few years ago they introduced a new hymnal into their denomination. This set of cassettes was produced to introduce congregations to this new book. The sound of these cassettes is the sound of a congregation singing hymns to the accompaniment of an organ. Some of the hymns were new to us, but that mattered little. Here was the sound of a congregation at worship which was very similar to the music of our own local church. These cassettes were what I was looking for.

From the second week of Walker's life, Stan and I played these hymns in Walker's hearing at least twice a day. Many times he went to sleep to them. Often he fed to them. When he was upset, these sounds helped to soothe him.

Soon he was showing clear signs that he enjoyed this music. These signs were never more clear than when we took him to worship. The sounds of the organ and noise of a congregation singing are clearly comfortable and comforting sounds to Walker. Walker has now been in many churches. Sometimes he has been in large gatherings where almost two thousand people have been heartily singing. Never has he shown anything but signs of pleasure when the sounds of hymns fill the air.

From the time Walker could crawl, he has pursued the red player around the house. Daily he would set out in search of the player. Once he found where it was located, he would use all his communication skills to tell us that he wanted us to play some hymns. He has frequently sat for up to twenty minutes clapping his hands and patting the player as he has listened to the hymns playing.

As I write this, Walker is almost thirteen months old. His taste in music has widened (with our help). Classical music, country music and Indonesian bamboo orchestras now figure in his selection of favourites. However, the hymn cassettes hold a special place; it is to these that he turns more frequently than any other especially at the close of his day or at the quietness of breakfast. These days when we take him to church, Walker can become fairly boisterous as he tries to compete with the preacher. So it is that each Sunday recently we have had lots of exits and re-entries. However, there has never been any trouble during the hymns. Using his own tune and his own time, Walker adds his voice to ours as we praise God in song.

On reflection, I think congregational singing is very soothing to the ear of a baby. It has a predictable rhythm and simple harmonic structure. It is free from sudden changes in volume or discordance or surprising variations which abound in other forms of music. Also, perhaps, the fact that it is made up principally of human voices in concert gives to it an added dimension of comfort to the young baby. Could it be that he/she senses it to be a universal lullaby, or a kind of welcome to the tribe or the people of God?

by Pauline Stewart

47

Sunday school, clubs and childrens choirs can help

The role of John the Baptist

Sunday schools, clubs and choirs must be like John the Baptist: they must constantly point their members past themselves to the worship life of the congregation. This is particularly important in Australia and New Zealand where few Sunday school and club programs extend beyond mid to late teens. The message which these organisations must give to their scholars should run something like this: 'Sunday school, club, choir is great, but there is something that is greater and that is the worship services of your church'.

This message can best be passed on by individual class teachers and leaders. These persons will make this a priority only when they fully acknowledge the limited holding power of their organisations. Leaders need to be aware that: 'Most children will grow tired of the Sunday school, club or childrens choir by the time they are in their early or mid teens. But once a young person begins to get the feel of the importance of worship, they have found a resource which will nourish them for all of their lives'.

To pass on this message individual leaders will need to:

Frequently tell children how much worship means to him/her.

Encourage children to go to worship and make going to worship part of the organisation's life — where possible preparing some contribution for the worship service. See the next chapter for suggestions.

Do all that is possible to minimise any clash between the demands of the organisation and the worship service.

For many Sunday school teachers, this will mean working to shift the Sunday school time from the same time as worship. In cases where it is beyond the teacher's power to change this arrangement, the teacher will cancel Sunday school on every possible occasion (Christmas, Easter, school holidays, etc.). On these occasions, the teacher will encourage students to attend the worship service and where possible arrange to meet class members and sit with those who do not have church attending families. This procedure could be followed by all leaders of children's organisations.

Beware

Sunday school teachers and leaders of Christian clubs and choirs who never themselves attend worship *are a menace*. By implication, they teach that following Jesus and belonging to a church have nothing to do with each other. Their influence in this matter of going to church with children will be counter-productive.

The special role of the Sunday school

The Sunday school curriculum at all levels regularly has lessons on the biblical basis of worship. In the older grades, this is supported with information on the history and practice of Christian worship. Most curriculums also suggest that worship leaders visit the class or the department. It is suggested that on these visits, the leader shows items of interest such as the communion vessels etc. These lessons provide wonderful opportunities for introducing children to the worship of their own congregation.

All lessons of this type should include a clear focus on how we do things in this congregation. This should include visiting the sanctuary at a time other than worship and giving the class a guided tour. Explanations given at such times will help children realise the specialness of the worship environment and something of the purpose of the gathering of the congregation.

All of this instruction can be supported by the development of learning centres. These can be used in church school, vacation Bible school and all-age celebrations. Twelve or thirteen self-guiding centres can be put together. A number of Sunday school curriculums are inadequate when it comes to lessons on worship. The learning centres can be used to supplement this inadequacy. The whole theme of a vacation Bible school could be on worship using the centres as the basis of the curriculum. Learning centres also work well in all-age gatherings.

Additional opportunities for this kind of instruction can be provided in the programs of vacation church schools, summer camps and family camps and all-age celebrations.

Other educational opportunities

If one of the aims of Christian education is to help prepare all of God's people for worship, then any time traditionally set aside for Christian education can be used for worship instruction. These settings are usually peer group settings with an occasional all-age celebration (a family night). There is nothing wrong with peer group settings unless they become a permanent substitute for corporate worship for all ages. Many things can be effectively learned in peer group settings: Bible content, church doctrine and history, the theology, history and practice of Christian worship. The following is a list of possible topics and ideas related to worship which could be covered in various church programs where children are present either in peer groups or mixed with adults.

Start childrens choirs or clubs which include worship instruction. For a church which already has a childrens choir or a club, the worship instruction program can be added. Following are some of the topics which could be covered in such a program.

a. How to use the hymn book. Your church's hymn book reads like no other book that children read. They can be instructed not only in how to read it but to find the author, date and composer of the hymn. While you are at it, you can teach them some of your church's favourite hymns so that the children will know them when they go to worship. A copy of your church's hymn book makes an excellent gift to children.

b. The order of worship. Take some time to go over your church's order of worship. What do each of the items in the order mean? Why are they in the order that they are in? Let the children write 'calls to worship' or prayers that could be used in a worship service. One fun exercise is to rewrite all of the items in the order of worship into sentence form. Each sentence should contain either us or God as the subject or object and of course a verb. For example instead of the 'call to worship' you could write 'God calls us to worship'.

c. Talk about the place where you worship and the furniture and symbols found in your place of worship. This is the time to take a field trip to your sanctuary. Let the children walk around and see and touch and ask questions about your place of worship. A helpful exercise is to prepare a 'treasure hunt' for children to match furniture and symbols in your sanctuary with items on a list.

d. Talk about the people in your church who work around the church. This should include both volunteers and paid staff. Who are these people? What do they do? How does what they do make worship possible? You can take the children to meet these people or have them come into where your choir meets. Let the children interview them about the work they do in the church.

e. Talk about two special signs your church celebrates, Baptism and the Lord's Supper. Again this is an opportunity to take them to the place where your church celebrates these sacraments. Let them see and touch the baptismal font and the communion ware as you talk about what the sacraments mean.

f. Offer communion preparation classes for children and their parents on a regular basis.

Creches, nurseries and crying rooms

All of these arrangements physically remove children out of the worship service. Some of them allow the children to hear the sounds of the service through a speaker system. In the case of crying rooms, the children can see as well as being able to hear.

In our view, these arrangements have a role to play in most congregations, but it is a limited role. We believe it is quite wrong to think that these facilities are for use by all of the appropriate age children all of the time.

Our whole stress in this book is that all children — toddlers and babies of church attending families — should be physically in the worship service. We believe that they should be there as often as possible and for as much of the service as possible. However, this is not to say that they ought never to make use of such a facility. Our view is that these facilities are useful for emergencies, for new families and for visitors.

There will be family emergencies when it will be sensible to use these facilities e.g. when a baby is in constant distress because of teething or when the supervising parent or adult friend is sick.

New families who encounter a church which welcomes the children are frequently surprised and anxious. They may worry about controlling their children, or they may feel sure that their children will interfere with their ability to enter into the service. For these folk, it is very reassuring to have a place to send their small children. Later, as they notice the pattern of attendance and behaviour amongst other families with small children, they will probably think again about where their children should be.

The children of visitors who have never been in worship probably need one of these facilities. No child and parent can learn to cope with worshipping together in one experience.

Most of the churches in which the authors have served, have one or other of these facilities. They have played a small but useful part in the lives of our congregations. But never have they been the places where most of the children of one age group are gathered. It has been our policy to work to see that during worship, most of the children of church attending parents of all age groups are in worship.

Is the church creche different?

Recently we were visiting a church. Half an hour into the worship, our baby's enthusiasm for listening to the echo of his voice could not be discouraged. So he and I exited. After walking him for a few minutes, I longed to sit down. I thought the creche might be nice for the two of us for a short while. Then I could still hear the service. On opening the creche door, we were greeted with a huge array of toys and two small children in a flurry of activity. My son almost leapt from my arms to a very large rocking horse in the centre of the room. I promptly withdrew from the creche.

There would never be any returning to the service once our little fellow perched on that rocking horse.

Our baby and in fact most children are not wanting for more time to play with toys. If children know that a creche full of toys is an alternative to being in worship, then no child will prefer to stay in worship. This is not to say that the creche cannot be attractive and welcoming. However, most church creches do not look any different from a playgroup room or a kindergarten. The same toys, posters and activities are found. Our suggestion is that wall posters, activities, story books and tools of play be more related to the environment of a church and especially the worship service.

For example, one creche had a large model of a church made of blocks. The roof was detachable and models of all the church furnishings were inside. Children spent their time in the creche re-arranging these furnishings and asembling pipe cleaner people to sit on the model pews.

Children's church

This term is used to describe a number of different things. With Catholics and some Anglicans, it means a simplified liturgical service based on the current Sunday by Sunday order of service. With other churches, it usually means an assembly of children in which songs and perhaps hymns are sung, the scripture is read and a childrens address is delivered. In some arrangements of Junior Church, children do quite a bit of the leadership of the service.

There seem to be a number of theories about the role of Junior Church. The Catholics have the best developed theory. Their Childrens Mass is a means of introducing children to the Mass and the meaning of its various parts. It is not seen to be a substitute for the real Mass. Usually the Childrens Mass takes place on a weekday afternoon. However, the children who attend the Childrens Mass are also expected to attend Mass with their families on the weekend. The childrens service is an introduction and not a substitute.

In other churches, the theories behind the various forms of childrens church are very fuzzy. Many Junior Church leaders see the arrangement as an alternative to the children going into worship with the adults. In these other churches, it usually operates at the same time as worship, sometimes for the whole period and sometimes for just part of the service. The leaders say that children enjoy Junior Church more than they do worshipping with adults. 'It is more appropriate and understandable' they say. The assumption seems to be that when the children are old enough to understand the adult worship, they are to move into the adults service. Junior Church leaders vary greatly in their estimate of when this time of understanding dawns.

This is a seriously flawed theory. Junior Church is not the same as the worship of the congregation. It feels different. It sounds different. It is different. It may be a happy assembly of children. But preparation for coping with and being comfortable in the worship of their congregation it is not. In some cases its effect will be the opposite. Prolonged exposure to the substitute can permanently turn the child away from wanting the real thing.

People who wish to prepare their children for a life in which worship is important to them must take their children to worship. They should commence this from early babyhood and continue it throughout childhood. There is no substitute. Only by exposure to the real thing will the children come to appreciate it and begin to learn to manage themselves in this unique environment.

Junior Church could have a role if it is seen in accordance with the Catholic model. This would mean it would have to take place at a time other than during the worship hour. It would also mean that in the program there would be a constant stress that this childrens service is no substitute for the children worshipping with their congregation.

When you tell me 'Jesus loves me' help me feel it

This song expresses the inner desire of children who listen to the Gospel stories and feel drawn by them. It was written for use in workshops with pastors, parents, Sunday school teachers and club leaders. Used in these settings, it is a telling reminder of the need for the parent, teacher or leader to love the children he/she would tell about Jesus.

HELP ME FEEL IT
Stan Stewart 1985

When you tell me Jes-us loves me, help me feel it, 'cause it's your face that I'm look-ing in to. When you tell me Jes-us loves me, help me feel it, As the on-ly way I'll see him is through you.

HELP ME FEEL IT
Stan Stewart 1985

Chorus
When you tell me Jesus loves me
Help me feel it,
'Cause it's your face that I'm looking into.
When you tell me Jesus loves me,
Help me feel it,
As the only way I'll see him is through you.

Verse
When you say that I'm forgiven,
Help me feel it,
'Cause it's something that I'm frightened to believe.
When you say that I'm forgiven,
Help me feel it,
As it's something that I really badly need.

Verse
When you tell me about Jesus
And I feel him,
Then deep down in my heart I know we're friends.
When you tell me about Jesus,
And I feel him,
I never want that friendship to end.

Verse
When you tell me Jesus loves me,
Help me feel it,
'Cause it's your face I'm looking into.
When you tell me Jesus loves me,
Help me feel it,
As the only way I'll see him is through you.

Optional verse
There are so many stories that I'm seeing,
Through television, books and video.
There are so many stories that I'm seeing,
Which ones I can believe is hard to know.

Children love to sing this song. When a childrens choir sings it to their congregation, the message is noted by most adults. Obviously the song's message is most pertinent to Christian parents and adults who are involved in ministry with children. However, in reality it applies to entire congregations, and especially to congregations who want to help children to participate in the worship service.

Chapter 5
Helping the children II
Appropriate materials and strategies for helping children and parents to cope with the fidgets and the frustrations which can arise during the worship service.

Andrew and Beryl wanted their two boys Stephen (9 years) and John (6 years) to come to worship. They had always believed that children should stay all through the worship hour.

When the church offered classes to help small children prepare themselves for communion, they eagerly took up the opportunity. The boys were glad to go.

From that point on, not only did the two boys attend the monthly communion services, they were also in worship every Sunday. At first, the congregation was glad. In this church, children were always welcome in worship. But soon the presence of this family of four in worship began to generate an undercurrent of complaints. The problem was the behaviour of the boys. They moved a lot and talked incessantly throughout the entire service. A couple of people said that they were hyperactive, unruly children. Wiser heads realised that the problem did not rest solely with the boys.

The parents of children attending the pre-communion classes were invited to attend some sessions with their children. Andrew and Beryl attended these with their boys and felt that they learned a great deal. They were relieved when they heard the pastor tell the children that he did not expect them to concentrate throughout the worship service. At question time, Beryl asked could children bring books and toys with them into the church service. Without hesitation, the pastor gave his assent to this idea. The discussion had ended there but in fact it should have continued.

On the first Sunday the boys were to stay right through the service, they arrived at church laden down with toys and games. This is the way it has been ever since. John and Stephen start playing as soon as they sit down and continue playing through-out the whole service. They play during the hymns and the prayers, the sermon and the announcements. They even play during the childrens segment. Nor is this solo play. The two boys play together. After doing battle with jet fighters, they will duel with robots (transformers) and then match their wits with a board game. All of this means that they never stop whispering (sometimes talking) and they hardly ever stop moving about.

In one way, these boys have been prepared for worship. They have certainly come to terms with the idea of staying in worship every Sunday. However, in other important respects, their preparation has been woefully lacking. They have not been given any guidelines as to how to cope with this time. They have not received any instruction on the kind of play and activity that is appropriate for the worship hour.

Because of this omission, the boys are in danger of upsetting the congregation that wants them in worship. Also, as long as the boys see the worship hour as a time for uninterrupted play, it is unlikely that they will receive much value from the experience.

Partly right can be very wrong

Andrew and Beryl were partly right. They were right in want-ing to have their children with them in worship. They were right in allowing them to bring toys and activities into the service. But they were wrong in allowing their boys to choose any toys and games that took their fancy. They were wrong in allowing them to play with them from the moment they entered the church. They were wrong in allowing them to play together. And yet Andrew and Beryl were doing exactly what they had been told to do in the pre-communion classes. The problem was that the instructions in the classes were not specific enough. If the pastor had taken just a little time to elaborate on this answer to Beryl's question, this potentially explosive situation could have been avoided.

Guidelines are needed

In this chapter, we will set down some guidelines which would have helped Andrew and Beryl and their boys. We have culled these from the experience of many churches. They are not iron clad rules nor will all of them be needed in every situation. But they are all sensible and workable and can provide a basis for thought and discussion in any church situation. The intent of these kinds of guidelines is not to restrict the freedom of children and adults. They are set out as aids which should increase the possibility that all parties will be able to cope with this new situation successfully.

Guidelines of some kind are especially needed in congregations and in families where going to church with children is a new thing. Once a family or a group or a congregation has crystalised its thinking then these thoughts, rules, guidelines should be shared with all the parties involved. This sharing should be undertaken with great tact and sensitivity. Unless proceeded with in this way, certain households and/or certain children will form the opinion that they are being singled out for criticism.

For instance, we know of congregations where a list of suggestions had been published and was given to every family. After this general distribution, they were distributed to newly arrived families as part of the general information handout about the congregation. Under the heading 'Suggestions About Worshipping With Children' these leaflets set out in a friendly informal way a number of points which are made in this chapter. There is more on this in the chapter 'Helping the congregation to welcome children'.

In other congregations, new people learn of the expectations about children in church through the pastor or through church visitors.

Some congregations have established norms of behaviour by using nothing more than modelling. It takes only a few families who set a consistent example of appropriate behaviour to set a pattern which others will follow.

In-church diversions — more than meets the eye

A few churches are against the practice of children being allowed to bring books or toys into the worship service. However, most churches approve of the idea and some congregations supply materials for use by children who remain through the worship service. We, the authors of this book, encourage parents and children to equip themselves with materials for use during worship. We also encourage congregations to prepare a work sheet as an activity for older children who are new to staying through the worship service. In our experience, most children will need something to occupy themselves for at least part of the service.

Some people find this approach to be contradictory. 'Why have children in worship at all if they are going to be looking at books and the like?' The answer to this lies in the child's ability to absorb many different impressions at the same time. As most parents find out sooner or later, children can be listening when they do not appear to be listening. Worship leaders note how quickly children look up when some part of the service or some illustration in the sermon is interesting to them. At times children surprise their parents by asking about something that happened or was said in the service when they appeared to be paying no attention.

Even when children appear to be tuned out or preoccupied by some activity, they are nonetheless tuned in. This is true of children in any environment. They are often aware of things that are happening to which they are not giving their direct attention. They are always aware of the tone of any gathering in which they are placed. So it is that the feelings and to some extent the meaning of a worship service is not lost on a child who sits reading a book or who is quietly engaged in some activity. However, its impact can be reduced by active play which involves another child — as with the story of John and Stephen at the beginning of this chapter.

Doodling and day dreaming that is different

The papers with which many congregations equip their pews can give clues as to what is going on in the minds of children during worship. Frequently children will use these questionnaires and envelopes as doodle pads. Many of these are taken from the building after the service. A few remain. For a number of years now we have been admirers of this form of pew art. In churches in New Zealand, Australia and the United States we have observed the doodles made by children whilst sitting in worship.

This pew art is seldom a random selection of scribbles. It is usually thematic, the most common visual theme being the cross, followed by nativity scenes. The most common written theme being love which is usually either directed toward God, Jesus or family.

Two stories

1 Recently I had the privilege of taking an eleven year old child to worship. This girl had never before been into a church.

During the sermon, I silently gave to her a piece of paper and a pen. She occupied herself with drawing for ten minutes or so. After the service I was able to study her art. She had drawn two scenes. The first was a picture of a woman dressed as a bride. I knew that the girl's mother had deserted her children when my young friend was only three years old. The second picture was a sketch of the inside of the church. Prominent in the picture was the cross. Below it stood a figure behind the pulpit. I do not know what is the exact meaning these images had to my young friend, but I know that thinking on these things during a worship service was a most suitable way to use her time.

2 A friend was sitting beside a small girl who was attending worship with her mother. During the sermon the small girl took a stewardship envelope and drew upon it. The mother who was engrossed with the sermon did not notice what her daughter was doing. During the last hymn, the mother caught a glimpse of her daughter's handiwork on the back of the envelope. Without looking at it, she reprimanded her daughter for drawing in church. 'You should have been paying attention' she growled as she hurried her daughter out of the pew. The piece of art was left crumpled on the seat. My friend uncrumpled it. The small girl had drawn a decorated heart shape. Inside its borders she had written 'Jesus loves me'.

Experiences like these have led us to encourage children to doodle and day dream during worship. This time and place which is set aside for the worship of God has an impact on children. The thoughts which run through their heads during these times are in the main serious thoughts. At their own level the children find themselves grappling with issues that lie at the heart of the gospel.

This is not to suggest that children are thinking like this all of the time. We are well aware of 'How much longer?' comments and the frustrated wriggles. But from time to time, these deeper thoughts are there also. Like the ebb and flow of waves, they move through the children's minds. We now believe that these kinds of thoughts are with the children in worship more than any of us had ever expected.

Just what the children think about in church depends in part on those who are sitting around them. This is not a reference to other children who may be nearby, but to adults. By their attitudes towards the children who sit near them, adult worshippers can influence their thought patterns. They can help the children direct their thoughts to peaceful and gospel related themes; or they can set the children's teeth on edge.

Provoking children to disruptive behaviour

I am an Anglican who married a Lutheran. He is a farm manager and his work has meant that we have shifted a number of times. In our first family home, we lived in a district where there was no Lutheran Church. At this time, we attended the local Anglican Church. During our time at this church we had two children. Following the practice of the church, the children were placed in a creche (nursery) during worship.

When the oldest child was three, we moved to another district. In this location there was a Lutheran Church that we planned to attend. On the first Sunday as we drove to church, my husband told me that this church would not have a nursery. When I asked why, he explained that it was Lutheran practice to have children in the worship service for the duration of the worship. The thought appalled me. 'The children will play up', I told him.

And they did. On that first Sunday they were all wriggles and complaints. I was terribly embarrassed. My husband just sat there as though nothing was happening. 'There is no alternative' was the only comment he whispered during the service. At the conclusion of the service, I was overwhelmed by the welcome we received. A number of the women were careful to tell me that they loved to see us worshipping as a family. The pastor told me that the children would soon settle down. 'Don't worry about them', he said, 'They are not disturbing me'. 'That's all very well for him to say', I said to my husband on the way home, 'They are certainly disturbing me'.

Next Sunday a number of the women of the church were ready for us. They welcomed us warmly and sat near us during worship. When my little one had an attack of ants in his pants, I glanced to see how my neighbour was taking it. She smiled at me and then at the baby. I glanced at others in my line of sight. They were all smiling. Their eyes were saying to me 'We are so glad you are here. We want to love you and your children'. Instead of being embarrassed I was deeply moved. For the first time I began to think that perhaps we could make a success of this attending church as a family.

Within two months, the children were managing in the service better than I ever imagined they could. What is more, they liked going to worship. To them it was like going to a big family in which there were endless smiles and many hugs. I am sure that this loving atmosphere helped my children to feel at home in worship. It certainly was an enormous support to my husband and myself.

Two years later, we reluctantly had to leave this area. Our next home was in a district where there was no Lutheran Church. Once again it was off to the Anglican Church. It was a similar kind of church to the one we attended in our first years of marriage. A creche was in operation and all children were expected to be placed in this facility during worship. The problem was that our experience had convinced us that our children could cope very nicely with the worship service. Also, sitting in worship as a family felt right. So we decided that despite the provision of this child minding facility, we would take our children with us to worship.

Now our children were the only children in the church. Whenever they wriggled or whispered, people looked around. Instead of the friendly smiles that were directed to the children and me in the Lutheran Church, we received disapproving looks and scowls. In a matter of weeks, the children's behaviour deteriorated. They started grumbling and misbehaving in a way they never had in our previous church. I am now sure that the children could feel the silent hostility that was directed towards them. It was this that provoked them to their noisy and disruptive behaviour.

The role of the congregation

People who disapprove of children in worship bring out the worst in the children. Children, including very small children (and we include babies) can feel hostile stares and disapproving looks. To them they are like sharp barbs. They react to them with all the noisy complaint they would have if they were sitting in a cactus bush. For parents in this situation, the negative attitude of other worshippers towards their children will create anger or panic or both. To say the least it will make their task of helping their child(ren) cope with the worship service many times more difficult.

On the other hand, adults who welcome children in worship can have a calming effect on the children. Through smiles, nods and winks they can help children feel welcome and at home in this setting. By eye contact, it is possible for warm adults to establish a relationship with a child sitting on the other side of the church. If the child becomes stressed or fretful, this relationship at a distance can help calm the child. The child's parents are also affected by adults who warmly support the presence of children in worship. The knowledge that they are surrounded by supportive friends enables the parents to handle situations in a cool and calm fashion.

The role of the minister

A supportive minister can do a great deal to help children and parents feel comfortable in worship. Many of the suggestions that follow can be implemented quickly and easily. In most cases, all that children and parents need is permission. The minister is in the strongest position to give this permission. Once this is clearly given in the presence of the whole congregation, it will help both parents and children feel more relaxed. It will also inform members of the congregation about their minister's attitude. They will see that families who are attending worship with their children are not flying in the face of their minister's wishes. It will help them to view going to church with children as something to be encouraged.

For congregations who have been used to worshipping without children, this is a revolutionary thought. Unless they hear the concept affirmed from their ministerial leader, they will have a hard time believing that it is a desirable development.

Materials which can be a practical help in church

Things to read and things to draw

Many parents and friends of children will bring with them to church books for the children to look at or read. Some parents specify that the child brings into the worship books suitable for the occasion. Books of Bible stories or those which have a Christian theme are obviously most suitable.

The activity which seems to occupy most children for longest (in minutes and over the longest span of years) is drawing. This means that a piece of paper and pencil are two pieces of indispensable equipment for adults who would go to church with children. As mentioned, children often draw, doodle and write on themes which are most compatible with the purpose of worship. For this reason adults who accompany children to worship should take a sensitive interest in their children's in-church jottings.

Toys and artefacts

Many a disaster has been averted by supplying a restless youngster with a spectacle case or key pouch. In fact, many of the items which an adult carries in pocket or purse will be of great interest to a small child for some time. Rather than leave things to chance, some adults actually choose to carry with them to church a number of small items which will be of interest to children.

Some children have special church toys. The paragraph on the church bag and the quiet book are extensions of this idea. However, some care must be taken when it comes to allowing children to bring toys to church. Toys which are very big or distracting are not suitable. Nor are noisy toys or toys which produce noise when banged. Small, soft toys are ideal.

A church bag

A church bag is a bag which a child brings to worship and which is only used on Sundays. In this bag there is a selection of articles for use during the worship service. This usually would include a Bible or Bible story book and it would also include a soft toy (or toys) paper and pencils, etc. Frequently a church bag also contains a quiet book (described in the next paragraph).

A child's church bag may be prepared by the child's parent or the child's adult friend or, in some cases, the child. In fact, at a workshop we lead on this subject, one mother shared with the gathering that, for her eight year old daughter and herself, negotiating and gathering the contents of her girl's Sunday bag on Saturday evening had become a very positive and enjoyable activity and had heightened their expectations of worship as a family. In a number of congregations, church bags are provided for all children in the church. The provision of the bags by way of a project has a number of benefits for the congregation as well as for the children. There is more on this in the chapter 'Helping the congregation to welcome children'.

A quiet book

A quiet book is a book made of cloth. It has sewn into its pages a number of tasks which small children enjoy attempting. The scope of these tasks is only limited by the imagination of the book's creators. However, these commonly include flaps to button and unbutton, zip fasteners and the like. These are usually made for the children of the church by a sewing circle.

A childrens corner

This is a kind of in-church creche or nursery. Rather than locating the creche or nursery outside the worship building, it is actually located within the church. Usually it involves removing a few of the seats (normally the back seats) and creating a carpeted space. In some churches, because of fixed pews, etc. the only possible area is a designated section of an aisle. In these cases it is important to set some boundaries, otherwise the whole length of the aisle will be used. Wherever the space is, it is usually furnished with some cushions and rugs. In addition to these, the area is equipped with soft toys and a number of quiet activities suitable for toddlers and small children. Where an aisle is used, this equipment can be kept in a clothes basket. The equipment can be put in place at the appropriate time and removed prior to the close of the service. Parents with small children keep an eye on this area, either on a roster basis, or simply by sitting nearby. Children are able to go to the area at certain times in the service. They can remain and sleep or play in the area as long as their play and activity is not disruptive to other children or nearby adults. There is usually an upper age limit as to who can use these areas (five or six years) and this seems to be necessary. These in-church creches will work best if the guidelines suggested beneath are followed.

An in-church library

A few congregations have set up in-church libraries of Bible story books. These books are suitable for babies through to primary years. They are kept in a cupboard within the sanctuary or on a shelf that is actually wheeled into the church after the service has begun. Children are free to move quietly to this resource and choose a book. Once a book is chosen, the children are encouraged to return to their seats with parents or adult friends. It is here that the books are read or looked at. Once the pattern is established, the library needs a minimum of adult supervision (over-seeing is more like it). The libraries usually operate only during the sermon time. Some of the libraries allow children to take books home during the week and others reserve the books for looking at during worship only.

Activity sheets and childrens orders of service

An increasing number of congregations supply children with 'activity pages' or 'childrens orders of service'. These come from a number of sources. Some are home made and others are provided by religious publishing houses. In congregations where a lectionary is followed, these activity sheets are normally based on the readings for the day. Other sheets are of a general kind with the activities based on a random selection of church and faith tasks. Completion of the tasks requires a pencil and some minimal reading skills are an advantage. The activities include quizzes, puzzles and drawing. Children who cannot read usually still receive the sheets and use them as they can, completing dot-to-dot exercises and doodling.

The sheets are usually given to the children as they enter the service. In some churches they are given out just prior to the sermon. Childrens orders of service are normally made available by the denomination's printing house. Both Anglicans and Catholics have a number of versions of these. These are given out at the beginning of the service and are used by the children throughout the service. Even pre-reading children are normally given an order (they are usually illustrated) and adults or older children help these smaller children follow along.

Guiding principles

There is a right way and a wrong way of doing everything. The principles below are designed to enable children and their church friends to obtain the maximum advantage from all of the aids mentioned. The principles are intended for use under normal circumstances.

Fifteen minutes worth of interest

It is unlikely that any of these aids will occupy a small child for longer than fifteen minutes at a time. This being the case, they should be held in reserve for use when they are most needed.

For instance, to illustrate the negative first, these things should not be brought into use in the first few minutes of the service. If this is done, their usefulness to the child will be exhausted in the early part of the service. This means that the child will face the second half of the service without the assistance of any aid to pass the time.

Here's how to obtain the maximum benefit from these aids.

Reserve their use until the part of the service when it is most difficult for the child to cope. In most churches this will be the sermon. A simple way of signalling that it's time to use these things, is to give out the materials (the quiet books, pencil and paper) during the hymn which precedes the sermon. Where a childrens corner is in place, the equipment for this corner can be put in place during this same hymn. With an in-church library, as described, children must understand that they have access to these books only at certain times in the service. With items like a church bag or toys which the child has brought into the service, another approach is needed. This involves encouraging children to leave these items alone until the time in the service when they find it hardest to cope.

Insist that children play quietly with these aids. Whispered exchanges between the child and their parent or an adult helper are acceptable. However, loud talking with other children is out of bounds.

Fighting or squabbling in the childrens corner can never be allowed. When this happens, it is time to take the offenders out of the corner and maybe outside until they have regained their calm.

Helping the children cope and join in at other times

Stress that the beginning of the service has many things with which the child can occupy him/herself. Encourage children to take an interest in the movement of persons to lecterns, the placing of Bible, the lighting of candles, etc. Allow them to look around the church and exchange glances and smiles with friends.

Encourage children to participate in the singing of the hymns. Even non readers should hold a book and all should stand. Readers should be helped to find the correct place and to sing along wherever possible. This should also be done with liturgies where responses are printed.

Discourage children from activity of any kind during the singing of hymns and prayers.

Expect that children will pay attention during any part of the service that is especially for them, or when other children are leading.

Expect that older children will set a good example for smaller children. This has force even with quite young children. Remember that even a four year old is older than a two year old.

Unsuitable in-worship activities for children

These include playing with other children and entering into long conversations with other children or adults. Unless for exceptional children and/or exceptional circumstances, this list should include sitting with other children without adult supervision. In such cases, the temptation to play, talk, pinch and/or giggle is too great for most children to cope with successfully.

Other unsuitable activities include playing with toys which are noisy or flash or which are visually distracting. An unsuitable toy can be as simple as a loud sounding baby's rattle.

Playing with guns or war toys is also not acceptable. Even though children might play quietly with these things, the associations which go with such toys are not compatible with the purpose of worship for young or old. Along a similar vein, books or comics which are on a war or violence theme do not fit into the worship setting.

Valuable short term help

In our experience all of these provisions are useful for a relatively short term — about three to six months. After this, most children will not use them. Instead, they will occupy themselves with self-made or self-brought in-pew activities. Or, where they have a special adult friend, they may choose to spend their time with this person.

Despite the short term nature of the effectiveness of these approaches, they can be most worthwhile. They are particularly

valuable in congregations that for the first time are working to welcome children into worship. These children will need some help to cope with the new situation. The provision of one or more of these activities will help these children greatly in the first few months.

The provisions can also make it easier for new people who have not been used to a children in worship pattern. The provisions offer to them and their children a half-way house through which they can be acclimatised.

There is one more most powerful provision which is most effective in helping children feel comfortable in worship. We call this 'An in-worship friendship'. This will be a major topic of the next chapter.

The Garden of the Mind

Boredom
is not defeated
by introducing another novelty
every time a person says 'I'm Bored'.
In fact, if you follow this course
the time will come quickly
when even new things
no longer excite
and life itself
becomes
nothing more
than
boredom.

Because
being bored
is not a state of being:
it has little to do with
the environment which surrounds me.

In fact,
being bored
is a state of mind.
It is a reflection
of what is within me.

Or to say it another way,
being bored
is not caused by a lack of colour
in the world around me.
Being bored
is the result
of a grey emptiness inside me.

Being bored
is life threatening.
It is destabilising
to young and old alike.

To escape from it,
young people flirt with danger and addiction.
Provoked by it,
adults run from relationships and reason.
The pain of it
fills small children with complaints.

But
the seeds
of boredom
are sown very early.
and once it roots
it is a weed
that's hard to shift.

Being bored
cannot be eradicated
in teenage years
by pool tables, hi-fis and video recorders.
Many youngster, who have these things
and more,
are chronically,
desperately
bored.

A strategy
to save a person
from being bored
can best be laid down
in the early years of childhood
when the garden of the mind
is being planted.

It is in these formative years
that this ecology of spirit
can best be nurtured
and provisioned
with resources
which will keep
parasitic 'boredom'
from entangling the life.

By love,
and by example,
by patience
and encouragement,
an Eden can be nurtured
within the growing child.

And
as it is established,
there forms within the child
a mind which is enquiring,
eyes which search as well as see,
ears which listen as well as hear,
and fingers which feel as well as touch.

As these things grow and flourish,
the person is made ready
to find
in all the changing scenes of life
the opposite of boredom.

by Stan Stewart
From *A People to Belong to.*

Chapter 6
Helping parents

Primarily a matter of motivation:
helping parents to see what is at stake
for their children and for themselves
then strengthening their nerve, showing
them how and providing them with extra help

Why do I have to go?

'Why do we have to go to church every Sunday?' asked six-year-old Joel as his family were preparing to go to church. There was a very distinct whine in his voice. For weeks now Joel had been watching children playing in his street as his family drove off to church.

'That's what we do on Sunday mornings. This family goes to church together every Sunday', answered Joel's father. So they went. As they drove past the children playing, Joel asked why was it that they weren't going to church.

'I suppose that going to church is not important in that family. But, it is important to us. And one day we hope that it will be important to you', said Joel's father. 'But church is boring', groaned Joel.

'I know it seems like that to you now, but I don't think it always will be' was his father's reply.

Predictable objections and unsatisfactory solutions

Parent-child encounters of this sort occur sooner or later in every church attending family. They usually do not end the way this one did. The encounter is more likely to end with the child winning the day — at least partially. In this matter most churches seem to aid and abet the child's complaint. They do this by providing at the same time as worship, alternative programs for children. Sunday schools, Junior Church, activity hours and nurseries full of brightly painted toys are all used to save children from the pain which they would feel if they had to go to worship. The churches hope that these programs and facilities will quieten the 'it's boring' cries. And they are more or less successful in this — for a while.

Mind you, most children attending these alternatives would still rather play with children in their streets or watch cartoons on TV. 'But', they reason, 'coming to this (the alternative to attending worship) is at least better than boring old church'.

The problem is that the alternative will only interest the children for a few short years. Then 'it's boring' will start all over again, and this time the child is bigger, smarter and more wise in the ways of the world.

'Why not come to church with us, dear?' the parent asks.

'Now that I've stopped going to the less boring part of church (the childrens activity), I am not going to go to the really boring bit (worship)' reasons the child inwardly. 'Oh, no thanks. I don't think that going to church is my thing' replies the child.

The parent may protest along the lines of 'Now you are older you will enjoy it'. But the argument is feeble. Their actions over the last few years of sending their child off to the alternative contradicts it. To the formative child it has implied 'Worship is too boring for you'. This notion leaves parents with nowhere else to go. Their child goes neither to the alternative nor to worship. If they are fortunate, he/she may still relate to a youth group or youth class. But usually this will prove to be yet another temporary phase, the attractiveness of which will probably not last more than three to four years. In fact, most children who have taken this route are by this stage on their way out of the church.

A strange argument, selectively applied

When it comes to going to church with children, many parents do give in to the wishes of their children simply because the children say 'it's boring'. This is a strange line of argument. It suggests that at four or five or ten, a child is equipped to make all the necessary decisions about what is good for him/her and what is not.

Can you imagine a parent responding to a child who refuses to brush his/her teeth in the following manner? 'I know that brushing your teeth is boring and I don't want you to do anything that is boring. What is more, I am afraid that if I force you to brush your teeth you may be turned off teeth brushing for the rest of your life. It's your choice. I am not going to insist that you brush your teeth. Instead I am going to hope that one day when you are old enough to understand, you will enjoy brushing your teeth.'

Or what about attending school for five days a week? How many children go through a phase — sometimes lasting years — of objecting to attending school? Then there are small children who, if given their way, would insist on riding unrestrained in the front seat of the family car rather than be belted into the safety of their car seat in the back. There are even toddlers who seem to feel that they can drive the family car and are deeply hurt when they are removed (sometimes forcibly) from behind the steering wheel.

Essential equipment?

Christian parents assert that belonging to Christ and his church is to be in touch with a life-saving, life-directing and life-enhancing force. Those who truly believe this must work to see that their children are also put in touch with this life-force. This must be a priority in their parenting. They should allow nothing to divert them from this purpose. This matter is too important to be decided by the whim of the child; by the standards of neighbours who do not share these beliefs; a holiday house in the country; Sunday sport; or even by a boring minister or an apathetic church. Parents who have this view will need to enlist the help of others with this task, but ultimately the responsibility is theirs. If belonging to Christ and his church is what they claim it to be, then at some future stage their child's very survival may depend on being in touch with this life-force.

Not loving but lazy

Parents who give in on these issues are not loving; they are lazy and delinquent in their duties. Parental love sees that the decisions of today must be such as will prepare the child for the future. In all of these cases the deciding factor will not be the child's present pleasure, but what will be good for the child in the long run. Pity the children who are allowed to decide for themselves their own standards of health care; what they can do and what they cannot; what is safe and what is not and the extent of their own education. Such children are deprived in the deepest sense. Similarly, pity the children who are left to decide for themselves whether or not they will grow up as part of their family's worshipping community.

Or excess baggage?

It seems, though, that many church attending parents view belonging to a church as nothing more than one of the niceties of respectable living. People with this point of view will not be influenced by this argument. For them, following Christ and belonging to his people is a side issue of life. Some church attending parents believe that their child's survival will depend on other things: education, sport, recreation and/or social skills. It is observable that these parents make sure that these things are always placed first in their children's life.. The actions of these families clearly show that belonging to Christ and his church does not figure in their kit of essential items for survival. Rather, to continue this metaphor, they teach their children that it is part of the extra baggage of life. Or is it excess baggage which they can pick up only if they have the time and inclination?

A hard principle to grasp

Going to church regularly makes a deep impression on babies and small children. It creates within them an enduring sense that belonging to the church and church-going is a part of their identity. Many parents who genuinely do see that belonging to a church is a central survival factor for their children do not understand this. They seem to think that sending them to Sunday school or some like Christian educational activity will suffice. They assume that these programs and experiences will be enough to prepare their children for a life in the church. Unfortunately, this will be so in only a very few cases.

Nothing less than involvement in the worship life of the church prepares a child for a life of regular attendance at such assemblies. There are no substitutes. Going to church regularly does not guarantee that the child will at a later stage choose Christ and his church. But it is one of the strongest means we have of preparing a child to respond positively to the claims of Christ and of commitment to his church.

For many parents, grasping this principle is one of the hardest parts of going to church with children. Once it is, and once the parents commit themselves to act on this principle, they find that the work of putting this into practice is more simple than they imagined.

Anxieties weaken

On the other hand, parents who are undecided on this matter are likely to have a terrible tussle with their children and themselves. Their children will quickly work to exploit this indecision. They will use all of their considerable cunning to subvert any church-going plans which their parents make.

For their part, the undecided parents are constantly plagued with 'should I or shouldn't I?' doubts. This lack of resolve saps their energy. Should they decide to experiment, they do so in only a half-hearted fashion. Such attempts are doomed to failure from the beginning.

The authors hope that through this book we can convince Christian parents and those who care for children of the central importance of going to church with the children in their care. Once this is decided they will put the matter in the non-negotiable part of their mind. Their children will come to class it with regular teeth cleaning, school attendance and a myriad rules about safety. They will know that 'attending church is a fixture in our family'.

At times, as with Joel at the beginning of this chapter, they will complain about it, but basically they will know that there is no way of avoiding it. Sometimes as parents insist on this pattern of family life, it may sound very negative. In fact it is very positive; it will re-enforce within the child the understanding that in their parents view this is an essential for life. They will sense that establishing this pattern has something to do with their survival.

Actions are not enough

The need for congruence

Going to church with children is not enough to ensure that they will come to feel that this is a positive part of their lives. The impression that this experience will make upon them will depend in large degree on how their parent or parents feel about going to worship. For instance, parents cannot expect their children to be more enthused about going to church than they are. This means that parents who themselves go to church out of a sense of duty alone are unlikely to deeply influence their children towards a life of church attendance. Children are experts in reading feelings. In most cases they will grow up to value what their parents value and to treat as trivial what their parents treat as trivial.

Here is yet another area in which parents must examine themselves. Here we will speak quite directly to parents. Parents, your child knows where you are at as far as the faith and belonging to the church is concerned. Your children are unlikely to want to go beyond your position — even if you tell them it would be good for them. They would rather settle for what they read to be enough for you. Many times, our children will actually live out our unexpressed fantasies — much to our embarrassment. Remember, modern children have little inclination to follow activities which their parents pursue out of duty. But they are as impressionable as any previous generation by whatever their parents happen to be passionate about.

Parents need to value worship

Suppose a parent finds that he/she does not really value going to worship, what then? If this doesn't bother him/her, then fine. However, such folk should not expect to make a success of going to church with children. But, if it does bother him/her, then there are things which they can do.

Eight things parents can do to strenghten their love for worship

1. Make attendance at worship a personal priority. Do not let anything interfere. Place it before pleasure outings, sport and home maintenance. If unexpected visitors arrive, invite them to attend with you, and if they will not, have them wait until you return. It is a fact that once you choose to allow something to cost you more, it becomes more valuable to you.

2. Take seriously the words and symbols of the worship service. By an act of the will, endeavor to understand and enter into the meaning of the service and to give more energy to your participation in it.

3. Work on your personal expectations of what the worship service will mean to you personally. Go to worship expecting that at some point in the service the love of God will confront you. Persons who have this expectation are never disappointed. This does not mean that they always hear scintillating sermons. It simply means that at some point in the service, and not necessarily through the flow of the liturgy, they will have an awareness of God's presence.

4. Prepare and strengthen these expectations through prayer. Include in your prayers the worship leaders and your pastor(s).

Ask God to use them to speak to you and the rest of the congregation. Throughout the centuries Christians have prayed in private for their public gatherings. These prayers are answered first and foremost in the lives of the ones who pray them.

5. Enter into the fellowship opportunities which surround the worship hour. This can greatly increase the significance of going to church. These human contacts become part and parcel of what it means to worship God. People who quickly run away after the service only rarely find any sense of being part of God's people. This has very great bearing on the way they hear and experience God's Word. Probably more than any other factor, fellowshipping before or after church, or the lack of it, decides whether or not the occasion is a 'cool' one or a 'warm' one. The simple act of deciding to stay for after service coffee can make a most positive difference to a person's appreciation of worship.

6. Reach out to people who seem lost and lonely. This should be a constant part of the worship experience. Many people complain that 'people did not talk to me' or 'they were not friendly'. This is a shame but it does not stop individuals from reaching out to others. You have it in your power to decide whether to be a receiver only or a giver also. When the decision is made in favour of being a giver, a person goes to worship looking for lonely or troubled persons whom he/she can befriend. Persons with this attitude are never short of people to relate to in any church. These helping relationships, usually become channels in which the help flows two way. These in turn become a helpful and exciting part of going to worship.

7. Offer your services on the worship committee. If there isn't one, ask you church council and minister if it is possible to form one. Being part of a worship committee will lead to a greater understanding of the liturgy. Through this you may become appreciative of some aspects that previously left you cold. Also, it gives you an opportunity to try and institute some changes. Remember, the first step in this task of any worship committee is to create a liturgy which enables the adults to enter into worship with heart and soul. Never start with the needs of children. The children most need to feel that this occasion means a great deal to the adults, especially their significant adults.

8. If the worst comes to the worst, go and find another congregation. Some people seem to find it impossible to settle under some ministers or with some liturgies. Their solution is simple. Change churches. Amongst the Christian communions, there are a vast variety of ways of worship. It is better to find a church to which you can wholeheartedly relate than to stay in one where

you are constantly ill at ease. But, beware of becoming a spiritual butterfly flitting from church to church. In the end that will help neither you nor your children.

All of these suggestions are made for the sake of your children. Of course they are also made for your sake. Remember, you are your child's most constant and most influential tutor. Also, note carefully, you are quite unable to fool him/her about your inner feelings. Nowhere has this more relevance than in the matter of going to church with children. If making a success of this is your aim, then the best gift you can give to your child is your own love of Jesus Christ and of going to church to worship him. Above all, you must work to keep this bright and fresh and quite up to date — yesterday's love won't do!

Preparing parents to go to church with their children

Many Christian parents do not need the previous section. They already love going to worship. In fact they love going so much they do not want anything to distract them from their participation.

Dena learned that the church she was attending was considering the idea of having children present during the whole worship service. The idea did not thrill her and her initial response was decidedly negative. She said to her husband, 'I am afraid our children would bother us and other around us if we took them to worship. Besides I don't think our children could sit that long. Personally, I love going to worship and I need the help I gain from it. It seems to me that this arrangement would make it difficult for me to get anything out of the service'.

Dena's response is typical. When the idea of including children in the corporate worship services of a local congregation is first introduced, it is often the parents of young children who raise the most objections. These are legitimate concerns and need to be taken seriously. Dena and those like her have a right to worship and to the benefits which come from this.

The church that wants to include children in worship will need to take the time to prepare the parents for their children's participation in worship. There will be fears to allay. There will be strategies to teach. There will be helpers to find. The following are some suggestions on how to help prepare parents:

1. Offer a class for parents on 'how to prepare your children for

worship'. Here is an outline of a possible course which draws ideas from the book by David Ng and Virginia Thomas *Children in the Worshipping Community* (John Knox Press, 1981). This course is designed for parents of first graders and any interested parents of kindergarten or elementary children. The course can be offered as a church school or study elective, scheduled over six weeks. The overall purpose of the course is to help parents to prepare their children for regular participation in worship.

Session 1 'What does the Bible say about worship?' The overall purpose of this session is to help parents formulate a biblical perspective on the nature and place of worship among God's people.

Session 2 'What does the church have to say about worship?' The purpose of this session is to help parents formulate a historical perspective on worship. This should take a specific interest in the historical development and current position of your denomination on worship.

Session 3 'What do I say about worship?' The purpose of this session is to help each participant to examine his/her own attitudes about worship.

Session 4 'What do children say about worship?' The purpose of this session is to help parents understand some of the basics of child development and to see worship from the perspective of a child.

Sessions 5 and 6 'How can we prepare children for worship?' The purpose of these two sessions is to explore some specific ways in which parents can prepare their children for a meaningful worship experience on a regular basis.

2. Create your own study session(s) based on this book *Going to Church with Children*. You may have particular needs in mind. At different times sessions could be held for: parents with pre-school children; solo parents and parents in a remarriage situation; grandparents (surrogate or real) and people willing to be helpers to children in worship; worship leaders and Elders or persons with pastoral care responsibilities. Alternatively, you can have a general mix of interested persons and parents. This mixing of interested people is most suitable for small congregations.

If you decide to do this, see that all of the persons you would like to attend receive a personal invitation (and reminder call if possible). Locate the event in a pleasant setting — perhaps a home, and build into it a time for coffee and informal chat.

Here are some clues as to how to create your own course from this book.

Select a story which is applicable to the group.

Read or tell the story to the group.

Have them comment on it.

Have them add to it their own stories.

Make a list of the problems.

Then read or in some way share one of the summaries from the book which relates to the story you have already shared. Have your group work on the points. Allot a point or two to small groups of three or four people.

Encourage them to

1. Examine the validity of the statement.

2. If they are uncomfortable with it, to write their own statement on the same subject.

3. Now they have a statement which they agree with, have them prepare a plan for its implementation in which they would be willing to be involved. Have them give precise definition to the first two steps and some vague indication of later stages.

Share the groups findings and action plans.

Conclude with prayer followed by an opportunity for fellowship.

Using this method, single sessions or multiple sessions could be designed. By placing the onus back onto group members, any impetus which arises from these sessions will have a local flavour. Also, such group sessions give the maximum number of people a opportunity to be heard. The hearing out of the parent's difficulties is an important pre-requisite for change, either in family practice or in an entire congregation.

Change comes slowly and is seldom without pain. For this reason it might be good to plan a series of such one night sessions — perhaps three or four in a year. It this is done, the evening could begin with some review of the progress made and the pitfalls discovered since the last meeting.

3. Set up personal appointments for those who have trouble accepting the idea of having their children in worship or who have special needs. This is a great opportunity to answer any questions and to provide help and alternatives if necessary. In some cases the child(ren) could be called in on these discussions. However, this should only be done after a discussion with the parents and should only happen if the parents desire it.

4. Promise the parents help and make arrangements for this help.

a. Train some older adults and others in the congregation to help with 'difficult' children. No parent should feel that their child(ren) are their responsibility alone. Help the whole congregation understand that the church is an extended family and that all the children of the church belong to all of us. This can be done in the context of any worship service, but is especially appropriate when there is an infant baptism. Allow children to sit with adults other than their parents in the congregation. Encourage all adults to sit with children so that they can get to know them and vice versa and to give the parents a break.

b. Provide alternatives. It is not a wise decision to try to legislate children in worship with no alternatives. Don't announce one Sunday, 'Next Sunday all of our children will be with us in worship for the whole time, no exceptions'. Provide alternatives for those who are still resistant to the idea or for newcomers to the church who are not used to having their children with them in worship. The alternatives can be an activity time or some other kind of constructive child care with church related activities. Make it clear that the child care is an alternative and that the church is working for the inclusion of all its children in worship.

5. Make your own handbook on 'Children in Worship'. These handbooks can be designed to help parents and other adult worshippers to consider the place of children in worship. They can make particular note of any recent statements or developments on children in worship which have arisen in the life of the congregation. They could also include an information sheet on the variety of children's activities provided in your congregation together with a list of contact phone numbers. These small handbooks can be placed in the pew racks; they can be given out to new members; and they can be given to parents who are presenting their infant for baptism.

6. Use infant baptism preparation as a time to introduce the place of children in worship to parents.

7. Offer a class on communion preparation for parents and primary age children.

8. Plan all-age events several times a year in the life of your church. The more all ages are together during other events the easier it will be to worship together on Sunday mornings.

9. Make available materials for family worship and help parents know how to use them. This is something else that can be covered in a class for parents who are bringing their infant for baptism. Most forms of worship presuppose a prepared congregation. What better way to prepare for Sunday worship than for families to learn to worship together during the week.

10. Send out an open letter to parents asking them to take their children to church and telling them why it is important to do so. A

sample of such a letter follows. This is only one approach. Having a group rework this letter to suit their own situation would be a wonderful exercise for a group gathering (see point 2). The letter can be addressed to the whole congregation or only to the families.

An open letter to parents

'You're not going to like this.'

I want you to take your children to church . . .

I mean into the worship service and to encourage them to stay for the worship hour.

'I told you that you wouldn't like it'

You have good reason for not liking it. As any educated person can see, having children in worship, especially small children, just doesn't make any sense.

'It doesn't make sense to . . .'

The parent

That's you — 'How can I worship with my children bugging me? I don't hear a thing and the worship hour is wasted. Besides, even when I am coping, I worry about the distraction they are for others.'

The congregation

'The children are so noisy. Their movements and grumbling take away from the atmosphere of worship. Some folk are already hard of hearing and they certainly don't need any further obstacles!'

The minister

'I breathe a sigh of relief when the children leave. It is hard to keep track of where you are going in prayers and the sermon, with noisy children wriggling around in pews.'

The children

'I'm bored! How much longer? Can I go out and play?' (Who can blame them? We know they hardly understand a word that is being said.)

There, that's proved it. Children in worship doesn't make any sense!

But parents . . .

I still want you to try it. I know that having children in worship doesn't make sense according to conventional educational theory. But what we are concerned about is something different to 'education'. My major concern, and I believe it is yours, is to pass on the Christian faith to our children. That is, we want them to grow up to be church-attending-Christians. That cannot be achieved by education. The Christian faith and a love of being in worship is *caught* not taught.

Did you know that having children in worship is important for all kinds of reasons for all kinds of people?

It is important for:

The parents

Yes, you. It is the clearest way that you can say to your children, 'Going to worship God with his people is the most important thing in our week'. It also gives you the best opportunity to teach them 'that in our busy week there needs to be a time when we sit still and quiet, and in wonder listen to God's voice within us'. Believe me, when you use example to teach these messages to young children, they go in very deeply.

The congregation

They are constantly tempted to think that belonging to the kingdom and living in the kingdom is a very adult, world-oriented thing. And yet Jesus said, 'Unless you become as little children you will not enter the kingdom of God' (Matthew 18:3). Having children around them in the worship service is a constant reminder to the congregation of this truth.

The minister

Clergy persons are prone to forget that the worship of God is important for all ages. It was never meant to be an 'adults only' activity. Having children in front of them reminds them of the simplicity of the gospel. Just by their presence, children draw the worship leader's attention to the fact that the church is the family of Jesus. This helps them to see that one of their main tasks is to build up that family.

The children

Although they cannot understand all of the words or symbols, the worship service speaks powerfully to children on a number of levels. For instance, it tells them quite clearly that worshipping Jesus is something for all ages and for all of life. It is a very special cultural experience which contains within it profound meanings. Children unconsciously sense that the business of this hour has to do with, 'Who I am', 'Who we are' and 'To whom do we belong?' Thus, a regular experience of worship can become a corner stone of the child's personal 'identity'. A child's experience of worship can be a time when he/she senses a special kind of love, the love and valuing of their larger family, their church. Few things are more valuable to today's children than this sense of security within a loving community.

Thank you for letting me have my say. I think I can hear you saying. 'OK! that's the theory, now what about the practice?'

Well, I know I am setting a hard task and most probably, you will not be able to do it by yourself. Parents, I believe that you will need help. If you decide to try having your children with you in worship, your church will work with you and for you to try to provide the assistance and support you will need.

Signed _____ and _____
                          Pastor   Childrens Ministry Person

Everyone needs extra help

Where did we go wrong?

The workshop day had drawn to a close. There had been the usual hurried goodbyes and then the rush to leave. The hall was now empty except for the two young women standing quietly by the bookstall. It was then that I sensed that they were waiting to talk to me — in private.

As they approached I recognised them as two of the most vocal participants. They came from a vital church and we had all been impressed by what they shared about their childrens program.

'We have a question to put to you which we find a bit embarrassing to ask', one of them said, 'You see, when it comes to matters of faith, we have a problem in communicating with our own children'.

'It seems so strange', the other burst in, 'our children's program is so successful and seems to be helping so many families. But when we try talking to our own children about prayer and going to church they don't seem to want to listen'.

'It wasn't always like that. Up until a year or so ago, we could talk about Jesus and say prayers with our children and our children liked us doing it. But that's all changed now,' said the first woman.

'Where are we going wrong?' the second woman asked. Her voice quavered with emotion.

What could I say? No doubt there were many aspects to this question. They went on to tell me about their children, four in all, aged between eight and thirteen. In all respects their relationships with their children seemed normal. It was only in this one area that they wanted most to be successful. And then there dawned on me, the one thing I knew which might help them.

'Do other people's children allow you to speak to them about such things?' I asked.

'Yes', they replied in chorus.

'With how much interest do they listen?' I asked.

'They seem very interested', the first speaker was quick to reply.

'Some of them seek out one or the other of us on their own. These children tell us their troubles and many times we pray with them', the second speaker added.

'Do you think that they share so freely with their own parents?' I asked.

The pair were silent. I continued, 'I have a feeling that some of them, and probably most of them, do not. You see, the problem you have described has been around for a long time. It is not just a problem of your families. Nor is it a problem of the 1980s. Children not listening when their parents talk about important matters of faith is a problem of the human race. This problem is as old as human history'.

Children need more than their parents (parent) can give them

One of the earliest pieces of hieroglyphics reads something like this: 'Young people are going to the dogs. They will not take any advice and they will not even listen to their own parents'. Let parents read and digest and be inwardly comforted. Modern time has brought with it a number of peculiar social problems, but there are still not many surprises when it comes to child/parent relationships. Most of the problems which concern us are really as old as the hills.

The women whose plight is mentioned needed to stop and think what a Godsend they were to some other families. Quite possibly they know some things about the children who came to them that their own parents did not know. Quite probably, these children's blood parents were also experiencing some difficulty in sharing their faith with their own children. I am sure that a number of them must have thanked God many times for the ministry of these two women.

What does this say about these women's own children? Nothing unusual! It just suggests that they needed to have a faith sharing relationship with an adult other than their own mothers.

I asked the mothers to go back to their church and look for some other adults to faith nurture their children. What their children needed was someone to be to them what their mothers were to some other people's children. Quite possibly, that special ministry was already alive and well. Frequently, it seems to be such an incidental thing that it can pass unnoticed under a parent's nose. But, for the child concerned, it is a relationship of vital importance and of great power in his or her life. Often, such a relationship is private with the child and he or she does not want to share with parent(s) its importance until such time as the child is ready. And that may be a long, long time.

None of this means that the mothers' early ministry to their children has been wasted. On the contrary; it is probably the most influential ministry their children will ever receive. It simply means that the children are at a stage in life where they have to run some cross checks. They need to listen to and talk with other people who speak about the same things that their parents have previously shared. In a way they are looking for independent qualification or verification.

By seeming to distance themselves from their parent's influence they are saying to their parents, 'I am me and not you. I must decide things for myself'. And what's wrong with that? In any family of faith there ought to be plenty of second mothers and second fathers, surrogate aunties and uncles, surrogate grandfathers and grandmothers to go around.

And perhaps there is an even deeper reason behind this childhood action of turning to others to check the validity of belief.

An ancient wisdom

In Papua New Guinea, everything has just happened. At the end of the Second World War, parts of the country were still unexplored and many of its inhabitants had never seen a white person. Some of the children of these recently discovered tribes have now been educated in an Australian university. These people have a foot on two worlds, one being on the world of their tribe with its laws and traditions which have not changed for centuries, the other being on the world of twentieth century Western civilisation where everything changes all the time.

Such a person was my gracious host. When the conference day was over, we would talk together about our shared interest in Christian formation and education. One evening, he talked about his life in the tribal village and of his recent visits back to see his relatives.

I asked him to tell me about the traditional stories. He told me of stories which explain the world's origins, and stories which explain who the spirits are and how people must relate to them. He explained that woven through all of these stories are the values and cultural mores which govern personal and tribal life.

'Have you told these stories to your children', I asked.

'No, I have not' was his reply.

He then went on to tell how tribal law forbids any parent from telling such stories to their own children.

'Who then can tell the stories to children?'

'Only the grandparents', he said. 'They must be told by the grandparents.'

During the course of the conference, I talked about these things with other people from different parts of Papua New Guinea and other regions of the Pacific. Although there were differences from tribe to tribe and region to region, some things were very similar.

I did not find one case in which the parents were the persons who were primarily responsible for telling the sacred stories to their own children. In every case, it was someone else. Sometimes it was an uncle or an aunt and frequently it was a grandparent or the grandparents. But never was it the work of the parent. I did not find out how many tribes expressly forbade the parents from telling the sacred stories to their children as is the case in my friend's tribe, but in every situation it was clearly understood that imparting this basic information would be the work of someone other than them

This practice is based on ancient wisdom. It is a wisdom not to be treated lightly. The method works. Using it, these people have passed on their culture intact from generation to generation for hundreds of years.

It seems that at its heart, there is the concept of 'mana', a concept known throughout the Pacific. Mana is a characteristic of some people. In simple terms, it is something like a combination of personal presence and the aura of inner power. When a person has 'mana', other people take note; when a person with 'mana' talks, other people listen carefully.

Mana is a gift that is often bestowed through the passing of the years. These cultures note that in the eyes of children, most old people have mana. They also note, that in the eyes of their own children, few parents have mana. Herein lies the reason why the important stories of the tribe must be told by persons other than the parents.

The cycle of stories which the grandparents and the uncles and aunties tell to the children are the most important stories they will ever hear. These stories will shape their lives and determine their behaviour. They are powerful stories; therefore they must be told by people who have special power with the children. They must be told by people who have mana.

The young and the old together

Young teachers/leaders may be skilled at arousing interest and imparting information. They may be popular with their class or group and serve them diligently. But these admirable attributes

are not to be confused with what the ancients designated as mana.

This is not an argument for replacing all of the young teachers/ leaders with old people. This would be neither practical nor desirable. Besides, dedicated young leaders bring beautiful gifts of ministry which the children badly need. Nor is this a suggestion that only teachers who are old have mana with children, but it is an assertion that most if not all teachers and club leaders could more effectively share the gospel if they had the help of an older person. The presence of older people in these situations will not automatically mean that a faith relationship will form but with a willing and loving old person in their midst, the chances are dramatically increased.

In this setting, the word 'help' is used very broadly. In a class or club, it may be as simple as having an older person who is known as 'our class or club friend'. This person may do nothing more than sit in on the group as often as possible. Perhaps the principal or only task is to chat with individual children as the opportunity presents itself; or perhaps an older person may come specifically to share a story or a skill.

In the worship setting, an older person could always have some role whenever children or young people are especially in focus. At times such as baptisms, confirmations, graduations and congratulations, a person who is visibly old should play some part. It may only be a small part such as shaking the child's hand, laying on hands or passing a gift. More confident older people are capable of making the presentation or saying a prayer.

The point here is that children need to see that the teachings of the church and of their parents are confirmed by older people. In a way they become our credentials. They authenticate the trustworthiness of the Christian gospel and the Christian way. By their presence, their nods and their words, they say 'Jesus is true. I've trusted him throughout a life-time and still at the end of my days I praise him'. Children never hear an older person say or imply that this is the case about the Easter Bunny or Luke SkyWalker. This witness has a powerful impact on children. It helps them to place thoughts about Jesus and his church in quite a special category.

Ancient wisdom — modern relief

One of the things that has come with the nuclear family is the notion that parents or parent must be all things for their children. That is not possible. It was never possible. Parents always have needed help with some parenting tasks.

In the church, with our emphasis on family life, it is often said that the parents are responsible for their children's spiritual nurture; often the implication being that parents must carry most of this load by themselves.

So parents brace themselves for this task. Often is has been a case of parents talking to children who have their fingers in their ears. Finally, as with the two young mothers whose story has been told in this chapter, they take up the strain 'Where have I failed?'

Behind many of these cries is the expectation that I must provide all of the Christian nurture for my children on my own. Ancient wisdom says, 'That is not possible. In our children's eyes you do not have enough mana. You must have help. And it is the responsibility of your tribe (people) to provide this help'.

Pa — a powerful presence in the kindergarten

Pa was very frail. One arm rested against the wall for support when he shook hands. Pa was doing something he loved to do; bid the members of the congregation farewell as they left after morning worship. He assisted the minister in this most Sunday mornings. Pa was eighty-three and despite the frailty of his body, the energy of his spirit seemed ageless. I had been the

guest preacher on this particular Sunday and so I stood with Pa to shake hands and greet the people. In the midst of this, a small child, about four years old, burst through the queue and cried out, 'Hi, Pa!' Her arms wrapped around Pa's kneecaps in an excited embrace. For a few brief moments, this little girl and frail old man were in a world of two. They exchanged some news, the child had a work sheet to show Pa and a kiss to give him. Then she was gone and the hand shaking and greeting continued.

'Is she your grandchild?', I asked when most people has passed through.

'No, I haven't any grandchildren. And no children either. I had two sons but they were both killed in the war,' Pa replied, sadness in his eyes. But it was only momentary. The smile and sparkle returned as he added, 'But all the children in this church call me Pa'.

I wanted to know more. Pa told me the story.

About two years ago, the kindergarten department of the Sunday school underwent some dramatic changes. The relatively small and stable numbers trebled in a very short time, far out of proportion to the families in the church. It was because of the high rise apartment blocks that had been built nearby. The community was no longer one of well-established and stable families. Many one-parent families lived in those new high rise apartments and they were sending their children to the nearest church on a Sunday morning — Pa's church. The noise made by all these small children increased dramatically and to maintain any sense of order became impossible. The two women in charge of the kindergarten cried, 'Help! We need some men'.

The first to be approached were the young men in the church. They had a lot of energy and seemed to enjoy helping with the youth group. However, there wasn't a volunteer amongst them. You see, to these young men, it wasn't a very acceptable thing to be seen playing with small children. Then they asked the men in middle life. But they were already too busy being chair persons, treasurers, stewards, etc. so there were only the old chaps left.

Pa continued, 'I asked the kindergarten teachers, "What do I have to do if I offer to help?" The answer was, "Come and sit". That didn't seem too difficult a task so my friend and I volunteered. I remember that first Sunday very clearly. It was not as I expected at all. The children were very quiet. My friend and I sat against the wall to observe and for the entire time the children turned around and stared at us. They were the stares of fascination. When the lesson was over, one of the little lads came directly to me and began to caress my sleeve, then my face as if he had not encountered anyone like me before. It was such a warm experience for me.

'The next Sunday, there were a number of the children who wanted to feel our faces and our grey hair. Before very many Sundays had passed, they were taking turns to sit on our knee and all shapes and sizes of oddments were brought to us as precious gifts. To this day, these children have not been too noisy or out of control. I've learned that many of these little children don't have access to a grandparent or regular contact with their father. My friend and I, just by being there and loving them, help to fill that gap. Last week, after two years, I told the children a story for the first time'. Pa grasped my hand and concluded with a lump in his throat: 'I think I'm living longer because of the children and I thank God'.

This testimony by Pa is far more than an account of sentimental exchange between some kindergarten children and two elderly men. What is happening in the relationship? Pa is loving the children. He is not teaching them but he is always there — to listen, to comfort, to guide. The children are loving Pa. They do not get a lesson from him, no Bible stories, but they want always to be near him and to share the important people and things in their lives with him. Pa's presence had an immediate and lasting effect on the behaviour of the children. As they became calmer and more gentle, Pa found his spirit to be energised and restored.

Pa's gift to the children has much to do with his lifetime of loving Jesus and serving his church and now being available to let that life speak, through his love and consistent presence with the children. Pa has that 'mana' spoken about previously in this chapter. The gift of the children to Pa has much to do with the Christ-like way they accept him and love him; ever reminding Pa of the nature of God's kingdom and of Pa's valued place in that kingdom and in Christ's service in his final years.

Building faith relationships

Pa and these small children have a *faith relationship* — a relationship where faith in Jesus Christ and a love for his people is passed on and nurtured. It is the faith relationship that is one of the basic building blocks on which to build congregational life that will help our children see and accept the love of Jesus for themselves. It is the faith relationship that has inherently the power to pass on a love of Christ's church and a commitment to serving Christ in the world.

Earlier in this book, there is the story of Mr Markwell, an old man who had a most significant effect on the strength of my own faith. We had a faith relationship. The point has already been made that parents are not enough for their children when it comes to matters of faith and that extra help is needed.

Most parents would value the influence of a Pa or Mr Markwell in the spiritual development of their child. Where and how do they find such people? The following points confirm the importance of these kinds of relationships and provide a basis for helping the children and adults in the church form them.

Faith relationships

a) Faith relationships don't necessarily form by accident. Pa had to be recruited following a plea for help. Mr Markwell saw it as his mission to visit our home and care for us over a long period of time.

The best way to find the valued help is to specifically approach an older person with a particular child in mind. Sometimes the parent does this on their own initiative or the parent will follow up a friendship that the child has initiated. More often than not, the parents will need the leaders of the church to help them. At the point of requesting any adult to form a special friendship with a child, there needs to be a commitment by the recruiter to encourage that friendship and to offer practical ideas in the early stages.

b) Faith relationships need more than the Sunday school class setting to thrive. It is through personal interaction — in conversation, the special outing, the birthday card, the phone calls, the home visits, the sharing of hobbies — that the child senses that this adult is very interested in his/her life and genuinely likes the child. Parents can play an encouraging role here by inviting this significant person to a meal, including their photo in the childs album, assisting the child to remember this friend at Easter, on their birthday and at Christmas.

This extra help cannot be totally provided within the time available in a Sunday school class or a Christian club. Without a doubt these organisations can help but extra time is needed. Nor is it fair to imagine that a Sunday school teacher or club leader can have a relationship as demanding as this with every scholar or club member. A few very resourceful people can handle two or three faith relationships; many Christians can only manage one.

c) Faith relationships are not usually formed between persons in the same peer group. We have sometimes lead a workshop where a participant will share the impact of a peer in leading them to Jesus and the church. However, most tell stories of a person much older than themselves. We have already emphasised the role of older people above. The task at hand for parents and leaders here is to see what opportunities there are for the children in the church to spend significant time other than with their peers.

The church program can encourage children and parents to foster these faith relationships through its programming. For instance, the publicity for a family tea or social occasion should urge every household to adopt a granny or grandad for the event. The program which follows should then find ways to acknowledge and celebrate the grannies' and grandads' presence in an appropriate way.

d) The most alert time for faith relationships is in the first five years of life. There is now no longer any debate as to the importance of the early years in the spiritual development of a person. Children are born spiritually sensitive and present child development research confirms that in these first years of life, the child decides the answer to these important questions: who am I? to whom do I belong? in what environments do I feel comfortable?

These questions are answered deep within the child at a very early age. These conclusions are reached long before the child can verbalise them. The data needed to answer such important questions is gathered by the child from the attitudes, feelings, sights and sounds of the significant people and environments in which the child is placed. The attitudes and messages of the parent(s), any adult(s) willing to form a faith relationship, the experience of church events, especially worship, are the major influences in the child finding such answers to these questions.

The power of the faith relationship when the child is very small must not be underestimated. Every toddler and pre-school child has the right to be given an uncle, aunt or grandparent in Jesus who will consistently love the child and open their lives to that child. Children *feel* what is important to an adult before they understand that what that adult says is important. The faith relationship is perhaps the single most helpful aid for parent(s) as they work at the task of bringing their children to Christ and into the church.

Chapter 7
Helping the congregation
to welcome children

Meeting the needs of all ages in the
congregation. Helping individuals to cope
with and contribute to the new situation.
Going the first and second mile of preparation.

The congregation is a kind of community. The attitudes which
this community has towards children will influence the experience of going to church with children. If children are thought of
as intrusions then this attitude will make things more difficult for
children and their adult friends. If the congregation welcomes the
presence of children, this will greatly assist children and the
adults who accompany them to feel at ease.

Adults who are used to worshipping without children come to
think of this state of affairs as normal. Once this pattern is established for a few years, people forget the children ever attended
worship. In these congregations, any attempt to re-introduce
children into the service is likely to be branded as a radical, new
idea. They have grown used to the quietness and predictability of
their 'adults only' service. They sense that the introduction of
children into the service will change this. And indeed they are
right, although their fears are usually highly exaggerated.

In these congregations, adults who wish to go to church with
children, instead of sending them to the childrens program, are
often thought to be 'unusual' or even 'difficult'. These folk find
themselves running against the stream of congregational expectations. They and their children may occasionally or regularly get
the feeling that members of the congregation are irritated by
them. This feeling creates a sense of unease in both child or adult,
to say nothing of what it does to the people who are irritated.

All of this means that a congregation needs to be prepared for the introduction or the re-introduction of children. A crucial part of this preparation must be some explanation of 'Why we want our children to worship with us?' The congregation must be helped to see that this move is not based on a parent's fad, or the novel idea of the worship committee or the minister. Rather they must be assisted to see that the step is being taken for serious and substantial theological and evangelistic purposes. Only when members of a congregation understand this will they agree to putting in the necessary work to see that this happens. The word 'work' is used deliberately. The introduction of children into a congregation will require effort and application from all members of the congregation who wish to see the venture succeed.

Worshipping with children is by no means fruitless work. The presence of children changes the nature of the worship experience in many positive and enriching ways. However, for most adults the benefits are hard to conceive in advance. Most will only recognise these after they have experienced them. Because this is so, congregations that are willing to work at going to church with children must walk by faith and not by sight. It is likely that they will have some difficult territory to traverse before they sight the promised land.

First steps and second thoughts

Neither Bob nor Alice expected there would be so much opposition. Bob was the pastor and Alice, his wife, was the Christian education co-ordinator in a three hundred member suburban chuch. For about three months, they had been working to prepare their congregation for the inclusion of children in worship. Prior to this the children had been present in worship on a few Sundays in the year and then for only part of the service.

The matter of encouraging children to be present in worship on every Sunday and for the entire service had been well aired amongst the congregation. At least that is what Bob and Alice thought until the theory turned into practice and real children began to attend morning worship regularly. When this started to happen, every Sunday brought new complaints.

Some people acted as though there had never been any special meetings, or announcements or notices in the bulletin. Others who went along with the idea in principle, found that worshipping with children around them was an uncomfortable experience.

Bob and Alice's experience is by no means unique. Any congregation that has grown used to worshipping without children and that seeks to reverse this trend will experience some pain. This pain will probably be more than expected. That is why there will often be second thoughts in congregations that seem to have been well prepared. In fact, Bob and Alice's congregation had a relatively low level of pain. As it turned out, it was pain with which they could cope.

Within six months, the complaints had all but died away. At the end of twelve months the children were a welcome and expected component of every morning congregation. This success was due in part to Bob and Alice's willingness to take their time in preparing their congregation for the transition. Equally important was the way they responded to the complaints after the children began to attend the service. All of the complaints were taken seriously. Wherever possible, action was taken to alleviate the cause of the complaint. In addition to this, Bob or Alice met with many of the complainers and related to them in a pastorally sensitive way.

Here is a sample of the people in Bob and Alice's congregation who had difficulty in coping with children in worship. They represent a range of personal situations and opinions that are likely to be found in any congregation. All of these folk have legitimate concerns. However, none of the issues they raise are insurmountable. The way in which Bob and Alice responded to these people is suggestive as to how others might proceed. Certainly, some work along these lines with these kinds of people will be needed if a congregation is to be prepared to welcome its children into worship.

The complainers and their complaints

Regina had been widowed for six years. Because she has lots of time, she has involved herself in all of her congregations activities for seniors. As is the case with many of her peers, Regina has recently experienced increasing hearing loss. She finds the movements of children distracting. But most of all she is acutely aware of any noise they make and once focused on this finds it almost impossible to concentrate on anything else. She says that this is the same for all of her age group. This is a generalisation but some of her friends have privately expressed similar concerns.

Apart from a number of heart-to-heart conversations which Alice had with her, two things greatly assisted Regina to accept the children.

1. Alice's request to the senior womens group for help. The kind of thing that Alice asked the ladies to do is set out in detail in the section 'The cloth book and the church bag'. Alice involved Regina in this project and this changed her perspective with respect to the children. No longer was she a passive, helpless spectator. She now saw herself as a helper with an important task.

2. Seeing noisy and distracting children being taken from the church. This had been talked about during the preparation period but many people, including Regina, never felt that it would happen. The removal of these children was a sign to Regina and many like her that their right to worship in peace was being respected.

Andy sells business management systems and does so very successfully. He knows all about efficiency and is often impatient with the church because of what he calls 'their un-businesslike approach'. His children Sandy (eight) and Shane (ten), both very bright and confident, have branded worship as 'ultra boring'. Jane, Andy's wife, would like to give the idea a try but after two Sundays of having the children with them, Andy had declared that the idea was counter-productive. 'It is unpleasant for the children and a waste of time for me', he declared. He sent a letter to the church council asking that some alternative children program be organised to take place during the worship hour.

When Andy's letter was read at the council, it was obvious that his point of view had a deal of support. However, the council did think that this suggestion was premature. They had previously agreed to give the children in worship idea a three month trial. Nonetheless, the council did two things which met Andy's request part way.

a. They established a library which children could use during the sermon time (see the description in the chapter 'Helping children').

b. They organised a childrens activity that operated during the sermon time in an adjacent building. This was a low key, low profile activity. When telling the congregation about this new activity time, Bob told the congregation that he hoped it would be 'for emergency use only'. Speaking directly to the children, he reaffirmed how important it was to him and the congregation that they come to worship and stay right through 'whenever possible'.

Andy's children immediately chose to take the activity time option. However, some of their best friends remained in worship. Due largely to the influence of these friends, after about a month of going out, these two children chose to stay in worship. On their voluntary return to the worship service, they became frequent users of the in-church library.

Bob talked with Andy but Andy was not impressed. But what did impress Andy was the fact that some action was taken in response to his letter. As the weeks went by he also noticed that some children were adjusting to being in worship more quickly and easily than he had thought possible. When his children chose to return to worship, their level of complaint was less and his level of tolerance had marginally increased. This enabled him to cope with a situation with which he still did not fully agree.

Jane tried to set up an in-church friend with whom the children could sit if they needed a break from their parents. But this never worked. Sandy and Shane never took to the idea nor to any of the persons suggested.

The Johnson family presented the greatest surprise. In this family the parents had attended the parents evening when the matter of children in church had been discussed. On the night, they gave their assent to the move and said they felt it would be good for their three children. However, apparently they changed their mind and began to lobby other parents to do the same. It appeared that the key figure in this about-face was their thirteen year old daughter, Amanda. Over the last year she had changed from a most agreeable child to a teenager who disagreed with many things. On hearing of the idea that children and presumably teenagers would be asked to attend church, Amanda gave her parents an ultimatum. She said that if they attempted to force her to attend worship she would drop out of all church activities all together. She had little trouble in persuading her younger brother and sister to take up supporting positions.

Bob and Alice spent a lot of time with this whole family. The resulting strengthening of relationships helped to soften the hard line stance of Amanda. However, she had made a stand and was not about to lose face.

To help her avoid losing face, Alice asked her to assist with the care in worship of a friendly toddler who was very prone to wandering. With the ready permission of the child's parents, Amanda became the toddler's minder. After a few difficulties due to her excess of zeal, Amanda grew to be quite effective in this role. Other members of the congregation noted the help she was giving and complimented her. This made Amanda feel good and feel good about coming to church. Once Amanda was happy, there were no further complaints from this family.

Barbara's complaints came as no surprise. From the time that the idea was proposed, Bob and Alice knew it would be difficult for her. She is a single mother with two pre-school age boys, the younger of the two being somewhat retarded. Her life is hard and her emotional energy is often close to being exhausted. For her, coming to worship is one of the brightest spots in the week. She enters into the prayers and listens to the sermons with a hungry spirit. All along she said that she feared having her boys with her would rob her of this important time of personal resource. She could see that giving children an experience of worship could be important for them. But she feared that in her case it would not work — and it didn't. She was embarrassed by her boys' behaviour and her own sweet hour of prayer was destroyed. Her hour of power had become another time of strength-sapping effort.

It was quite clear that the solution to Barbara's problems would be to find an in-church friend for her children. When this was first suggested to Barbara, she would have none of it. She felt that to accept this kind of help would be a poor reflection on her ability as a mother. 'She would cope like everyone else', she said.

What eventually helped her most was the example of other parents. Several of the two parent families had successfully nurtured the in-church friend idea. Watching their children relate to their church friend helped her to see that this was a good arrangement that in no way reflected ill on the parents. This meant that when Alice asked her again about having an in-church friend, she agreed to give the arrangement a try.

Alice chose a retired couple whose own grandchildren lived far away. They needed some encouragement as they were apprehensive of the retarded child. However, once they had met Barbara and her children socially on a couple of occasions their hesitancy evaporated. The children took to the couple and were especially fond of the man.

The children continued to sit with Barbara for most of the service, but they would always have one or two periods of sitting with their church-grandparents. On occasions when restlessness would overcome one of the children, it was usually one or other of this older couple who would take the child out. Within a few months, Barbara and her children and their relationship with this couple was one of the success stories of the move to have children in worship.

Going the second mile

In some congregations, what has just been described is the second stage of preparation. This was the case in Bob and Alice's church. The program of preparation through which they had taken their congregation was the first stage. This chapter has commenced with the second stage first, to stress its importance. Thorough preparation before the event is never enough. In this matter, there is always a second mile to walk. What happened with Bob and Alice is simply an outline of the kind of things which can be entailed in walking this second mile. People who feel that there is only one stage to this process will generally be sadly disappointed. Those who would prepare a congregation to accept children must have enough energy and determination to walk both miles of this journey.

Wrong attitudes in relation to children in worship are like temptations. They just keep coming back. This is because of the way we are all constantly massaged by our culture and our times. Constantly we are being force-fed with values and attitudes. Imperceptibly, they shape us. Going to church with children runs completely contrary to most of these values and attitudes. Persons and congregations who commit themselves to this course must steel themselves for the inevitable bombardment they will have from contradictory notions.

A good education and publicity program may help rouse a congregation's determination, but it will only do that for a short time. Backsliding can come at an alarming rate. Often this is fuelled by new members who have never encountered the practice before. Children grow older and adults enter a new lifephase and find a different perspective. These factors and many others soften up a congregation's resolve.

Therefore this matter of helping a congregation positively to welcome children and their adult friends into worship is work that never ends. It must be a matter of continuing education. With this in mind, personal objections and difficulties should be welcomed. They provide further opportunities to keep on the case. They give reasons to reiterate what is at stake. They give cause for discussing and demonstrating basic principles with the person concerned and in the caring groups of the congregation.

The first mile
A suggested outline of a program to prepare a congregation to welcome children and their adult helpers into worship

The following steps, or some variation of them, have been used by congregations that have been used to worshipping without children present. Most of these churches have had some kind of childrens program running at the same time as worship, either for the duration of the service or for part of the service. In these cases, encouraging children into worship has meant either rescheduling the childrens activity or downgrading it to the position of being a minor option.

To work effectively any program of preparation needs to have a ground swell of favorable opinion to build upon. This may comprise three or four parents who are willing to try worshipping with their children. It may come from Sunday school teachers who feel that Sunday school at the same time as church is unsatisfactory.

It this ground swell does not exist except in one enthusiast, it is probably best for this one person to gossip the gospel. By this is meant that the person shares his/her enthusiasm informally whenever the opportunity presents itself. This can include sharing articles and books like this one. Once a person starts this ferment, it will not be long before he/she finds others who are interested in the concept. A number of things are happening within and outside the church that are pushing people to think about similar things. Many notions on bonding and the like that float in and out of the media will lend weight to anything an enthusiast does. Once discussion and thought is stirred up, the sole enthusiast for going to church with children should not be lonely for long.

1. Meeting with the concerned persons
Obviously church attending parents will be of foremost importance in any discussions. However, there are others who are also vitally concerned: these include Sunday school teachers, club leaders, grandparents and any other adults who have a special concern for the children of the congregation.

In cases where Sunday school or some other program is operating at the same time as church, there must be prior consultation with the leaders of these organisations. Obviously, any move to encourage children to stay in the worship service will effect their attendances. Many leaders will welcome this; some will not. This is an area in which to tread carefully. These folk will need to be reassured that the move is not a reflection on their competence. All leaders will have to be helped to understand the motivation that lies behind the move.

Even when Sunday school is operating at a different time to worship, care should be taken to inform fully the teachers of any drive to have children in worship. If teachers understand the reason why this is being done, they can use their influence to encourage children and parents to worship together. If they do not understand, then their influence might unintentionally be to discourage attendance.

The decision as to who should be invited to a meeting will probably depend on the numbers involved. In a very large church, it might be wise to gather the parents in separate groups according to the ages of their children. In smaller churches, all parents, Sunday school teachers, leaders and other interested adults could be gathered in the one meeting.

There are a number of suggestions on the subject matter of a meeting in the chapter 'Helping parents'. In Appendix I there is a section entitled 'The ten commandments of children in church'. Composing such a document as a group task could be a way of opening up the whole subject and of sharpening ideas.

If this meeting is to lead to a church-wide education and publicity program, three things should emerge from the first meeting.

a. A desire for further meetings. Perhaps a course as outlined in the chapter on helping parents.

b. A report to be sent to the congregation's council. The aim of this is to allow for a sharing of the opinions of the meeting and to provoke further discussion. This could contain some proposals with reference to a publicity education program.

In some cases these proposals should also contain suggestions as to allocating a new time to the Sunday school program or other activities that clash with worship.

c. A suggestion that a committee be formed to work on the proposals with a list of names of persons who would be willing to be committee members.

2. A study and discussion process

From here on it is assumed that the congregational council has given its approval to an education and publicity campaign.

3. A course of study

The people who are most likely to be willing to undertake some study on this are the parents and children's teachers and leaders. People organising such courses should be ready for disappointments and surprises. Some folk who should attend, won't attend and others who have never attended study sessions may choose to attend.

4. Sharing and discussion

Choose a few people who can share the concept with competence and clarity. Request that every group in the church, e.g. mens, womens and youth, give some opportunity for one of these folk to share what is being proposed. A group may choose to allocate an entire evening for sharing and discussion on this topic. Most groups will be able to make available a ten minute spot only. Nonetheless this time is sufficient to raise the issue and answer a few questions.

In most churches it will take two to three months to cover all of the groups in this way.

The role of the minister(s)

Some ministers choose to have no role whatsoever in any move of this sort. They distance themselves from the endeavour and leave it to the lay enthusiasts. When ministers take this stand, they seem to be motivated by either sloth or fear. The slothful ones do not like the idea of all of the extra work this will entail; and it's true that bringing children into worship will make their task more difficult. The fearful ones are afraid that the presence of children will wreck their liturgies and rob worshippers of its meaning. Some are fearful of the negative reactions to the presence of children from members of their congregations.

People who are in congregations where the minister stays aloof from this issue should not think that nothing can be achieved. If lay people are enthusiastic enough, an entire publicity and education program can be mounted. Obviously, it will be more difficult than in cases where the minister does give support, but some progress is possible. Often when a non-committal minister sees that some progress is being made, he/she will then become quite supportive.

Thankfully an increasing number of ministers are willing to support moves to bring children into worship. However many of these remain tentative about the idea. They would like it to work but are not sure that it can. A few ministers are out and out enthusiasts for children in worship and are willing to spearhead any moves in this direction.

Any support that the minister can give in his/her role as a worship leader will be helpful. Ministers who are convinced on this matter will find no shortage of opportunities to refer to it in their routine preaching and teaching. All sympathetic ministers will find that their weekly readings often present them with helpful pointers that they can bring to their congregations' attention. The words and works of Jesus and the Pauline symbols for the church provide many of these.

Helping families prepare themselves to worship together fits naturally into a minister's pastoral role. In many cases, people who have problems with the idea will seek out the minister. These discussions provide opportunity for the minister or — at the minister's direction — for some other person to talk directly with the concerned person. The minister can also inform people who are new to the parish of developments in this field and what it is hoped will be achieved.

The minister's opinion at church councils and at pastoral care meetings will be noted by many people. His/her willingness to work towards bringing the children into worship will encourage many others to at least give the idea a try.

The minister can aid the cause of children attending worship by talking to the children in the context of worship. If the minister especially welcomes the children into worship, he/she helps the congregation to do the same. At times the minister will be the person in the best position to say some word of caution to the children about noisy or distracting behaviour. When this is done in a loving and firm way, it will prove to be very helpful to the children; it is just as helpful to the congregation. It helps them to realise that the situation which is being encouraged is not 'children present at any price'. But rather one in which 'children always welcome, but reasonable behaviour is expected of them'.

The way a minister relates to children will be noted by his/her congregation. This being the case, a minister who wishes to help his/her congregation welcome children should make the most of every contact with children. This is particularly important in relation to his/her contacts with children, before and after and during worship. When a minister consistently greets children in a warm and personal way, he/she is setting an example which many lay people will follow. Through this warm relationship with children, the minister is telling the congregation 'It is good to have the children here with us. I am pleased that they are here and you should be also'.

However, not even the most enthusiastic minister can bring the children into worship without ground swell support. This move can never work on the basis of the vision of one person — not even if that person is the minister.

Talking with the children

Some people suggest that the children be asked their opinion about being in worship. This is a naive suggestion. Few children of an age to understand such questions would ever choose to be in worship. Children of this age would almost always prefer some play or educational activity over being present in a worship service. Of course, given a wider choice still, most children would rather be watching cartoons than being regularly involved in any kind of Christian program. Children are as likely to choose to worship regularly as they would be to choose to clean their teeth regularly or to go to school regularly.

The decision as to whether or not a child should go to church regularly is one of those decisions that must be taken by the parent on the child's behalf. It is only one of the many decisions that every parent must make for his/her children. In regard to faith formation and the creation of a consciousness of belonging to God's family, it is one of the most important.

However, this does not mean that children be ignored in this process of preparing to go with them to church. There are many things that need to be discussed with them; their opinions and suggestions should be carefully considered. But the one thing they should be clear on, is that their opinion on whether or not they attend is not being called for.

Talking with children who are soon to move into worship can take place in groups or in the setting of their family. In some cases, as with the Johnson family, there is no alternative to spending time with the family. Whether in a family setting or in a group, it is suggested that the first meeting with the children be without the parents present. Parents can be invited to listen and participate in a second meeting.

How to talk to children

When a church or family decides to switch from taking their children out of worship to bringing them into worship, the children will need to be patiently talked with.

Children will need to know:
>   why this move is important to them;
>   why it is important to the congregation;
>   what provisions will be made to help them cope;
>   what part they can play;
>   what the various parts of the service mean.

Children need to talk about:
>   the things they feel they will find most difficult;
>   their suggestions as to provisions which could be made to help them with the service;
>   the things in the service they do not understand.

Children need to be reassured:
>   that if they have trouble coping or somehow behave inappropriately, that they will be treated with patience; that help will be provided and that wrong behaviour will be forgiven;
>   that on occasions there will be lots of interesting things for them to do and to interest them in the service;
>   that many adults will be very pleased to see them in worship and will welcome them.

Generally, the older the child the more difficulty he/she will have in making a switch from being in a childrens activity to being in worship. These children deserve the most sympathy and should be given lots of support.

Note that all of the above assumes that at least one parent or one close adult friend intends to go with the child(ren) of each family to worship. The approach will be ineffective with children who lack an adult who is committed to going to church with them.

Gathering the resources

Children are going to need help, particularly in the early weeks. The kind of things which can be provided are listed in the chapter 'Helping children'. Do not over supply these. Try one or the other but not all at once. This means that if one fails to meet the children's needs, there are other alternatives which can be quickly put into place. And remember, most children will adapt quickly to the worship setting. After a few months, maybe as few as two, many children will find their own way of coping with the service. They can do this without any assistance by way of aids especially provided by their church. However, without any doubt, some kind of physical assistance by way of aids must be supplied for children the first time they attend worship for the whole time.

An area in which great care must be taken is in the provision of people resources. Most children will benefit from a special in-church friend. Indeed, some children and some families will simply not be able to cope without some back-up relationship from day one. Most commonly the children who will need this help from the beginning are those who come from solo parent households.

During this preparation phase, some of the organisers should examine the list of families who will participate. From this the children and families who are most likely to need help should be identified. Then it will be a matter of attempting to match the children of these families with adult friends. In many cases, this will mean nurturing a relationship from scratch. Often, as in the case of Barbara in this chapter, this process will not work at the first try. But if it is persevered with, some helpful relationships should come into being. There is more on this in the chapter 'Helping the children II'.

Planning the first month

Almost inevitably, any move to bring children into worship will be for a trial period only. Many people will adopt a 'wait and see' stance. Some will expect the initiative to fail; a few may be hoping that it fails. This means that the first month that the children are in worship is a very critical time for the success of the entire venture. A couple of disasters in this period can put a premature end to the whole idea. Once this happens, opinion in the congregation will become so fixed that children in worship will become a closed subject, and it is usually years before the subject can be broached again.

A plan is needed to cover the first month to help ensure the smooth introduction of the idea and to keep disasters at bay. This plan should cover such items as the provision of resources mentioned above with attention to practical detail of how they will be supplied and distributed and where they will be located, etc.

There should be some involvement of children in the worship service. Note that this involvement may be in quite small ways. Somehow in this first month the message must be put across that children are welcomed here and that children can help with the worship of God. Go carefully. Hasten slowly and do not attempt too much too soon.

Even children who come with adults often do not know how to behave in the pre- and post-worship periods. Noisy or distracting behaviour at these times can be held against them and the idea of their inclusion in worship. This can easily happen in these first weeks as the result of the children slipping away from their adult companions and congregating together.

Some enthusiasts for the children in worship should hold themselves ready to quieten tactfully any children who become over excited in this way. They should do this in such a way as to set an example that other caring adults (the adults the children came with and others) can follow. Other adults will feel that what they have seen modelled before them has given them permission to act also. When this happens, the child feels that the whole worshipping community is requesting that he/she act and speak quietly. This type of community expectation has a powerful influence on children.

A plan needs to be formulated as to what can be done to help a parent and child who are clearly not coping. It should be borne in mind that some adults freeze when the child in their care starts to act up in a public place. They seem to be completely unable to make any response to quieten their child and consequently their child's actions grow worse. On the other hand, some parents seem oblivious to their child's behaviour even when it is distracting an entire congregation. One (or both) of the situations described is likely to happen in the first month. The planning committee should think out in advance how they can sensitively tackle the situation and defuse it before it becomes a major incident.

A review arrangement

This chapter opened by talking about the necessity of going the second mile. Just what this second mile will comprise will only become evident once the children begin to come to worship. Therefore it is necessary that the committee that has piloted the project thus far set up some kind of review process to check progress and problems. It will not be enough for this to be done after a long period, for instance three months. If it is left this long, some situations will become so difficult as to be virtually unfix-able. In the early stages of this initiative, it will need to be done week by week. In this way persons who are not coping or situa-tions which are causing aggravation can be attended to that week. A prompt personal response and positive corrective actions are essential to the success of this kind of venture. As the problems of the first weeks are ironed out, then the committee need only meet to review developments as occasion requires.

Most congregations will ask that the whole matter be reviewed at a congregational meeting at the end of a trial period, usually six months. If nothing has been done by way of reviews as men-tioned in the previous paragraph, then this meeting will probably see an outpouring of complaints. These in turn could well lead to the immediate re-institution of high profile, during worship childrens activities. On the other hand, if the reviews mentioned above have been leading to effective action, then most of the sore spots will have been dressed as they arose. In these cases, the idea of children in worship will have won a good deal of congre-gational support. As a result it will be accepted by the meeting as a desirable pattern of worship which should continue.

Appendix I
The ten commandments of children in our church

A congregation's confession of faith

A congregation needs to make up its mind about its attitude towards children in the worship service. Most have never thought much about it. More often than not, they will find that expediency has been the force that has shaped their current practice. Should a congregation seek for advice on this matter from some higher churchly authority, they are unlikely to receive any. In recent times, few bishops or courts of the church have had anything of a practical and detailed nature to say about the place of children in Sunday by Sunday worship. Obviously, then, this is an issue which has to be decided congregation by congregation.

Perhaps this is all to the good. This situation forces congregations to make up their own minds on this crucially important issue. When a congregation responds to this challenge, the members embark on a course which will cause many of them to do some very personal and pertinent theologising.

The usual way for a congregation to prepare a statement on anything is to appoint a committee to produce a first draft. This is a most sensible first step in regard to a question such as 'What is our congregation's attitude towards children in worship?' The first question any such committee will face will be 'Where do we start?'

Set out in this appendix is a statement entitled 'ten command-ments for children in worship'. We (Stan and Pauline Stewart) prepared this to be a first step in the work of such committees. Our idea is that a local congregational committee could take the statement point by point, question it and rework it to suit their own view point. In doing this they will cover most of the crucial areas that must be addressed if this question is to be adequately answered. The end of this process will be a relatively short statement which they can then present to their council. After further refining by their council and any other groups who need to be consulted, it can then be finalised. Once this is done, the congregation has its very own policy statement on children in worship.

The value of the statement is as much in the preparation as the end result. All of the people who have questioned or discussed it have had to think about the issues involved. By the time the statement is ready for release there will be a heightened awareness in the congregation of all matters related to children in church. It is doubtful if any pronouncement coming from outside the congregation could ever stir up so much thought on this important subject.

No statement of this kind will ever be the final word. But it can be a useful stage on the way. When further revisions are needed, these can be prepared by using the method used to produce the first draft.

Once the agreed statement is on hand, share it with your congregation. Give all worshippers a copy and have one or two people speak about it briefly. If the statement comes out of a process of preparation to welcome children into worship, it could be given out as the culmination of this period.

After it has been launched, be sure to have it displayed on notice boards in the church porch and in the Sunday school hall. Also keep copies on hand to be given to new families as they arrive.

Ten commandments for children in church

1. Thou shalt love your children. Your children are part of the church of today. They are not to be kept in cold storage for the church of tomorrow. They have not been sent by the devil to distract you but by God to enrich you.

2. Thou shalt endeavour to form particular friendships with one or two children who are beyond your owr blood family circle. Where possible, their relationship with you shall extend beyond in-church contact to informal social contact at other times and places. Thou shalt always remember that the friendship of your child's friends is as important for your own spiritual development as it is for their well-being.

3. Thou shalt encourage your children to worship with your congregation and value their presence in these gatherings. Thou shalt recognise that, by their presence, your babies, toddlers and children have much to contribute to the atmosphere of worship. Thou wilt be open to the possibility that God can speak to you through their smiles, their questions, their embraces, their wriggling and their responses.

4. Thou shalt extend to thy children a warm, personal and appropriate welcome when they come to worship. As they leave, you shall bid them an affectionate farewell. Thou shalt have within each worship service a sign that children are welcome.

5. Thou shalt allow children to participate in the leadership of worship as frequently as practicable. However, thou shalt not make an undue fuss over their participation, nor exalt their contribution above that of other age groups. Your children shall know that the leadership of worship is a 'team' task which is to be shared by all the age groups in their Christian family.

6. Thou shalt not allow your children to regularly run riot in worship. However, thou shalt not leave the responsibility of quietening the children to their parent(s) alone. All members of the congregation will by word, deed and spirit encourage in the children a calm and reverent frame of mind and quiet and appropriate movements.

7. Thou shalt make much of the festivals of the Christian year and other special occasions. On these occasions thou shalt be sure to enable your children to bring their brightness through their participation, their artistic contributions and where possible, their leadership.

8. Thou shalt not expect your children to be more enthusiastic about the worship of your congregation than you are. Nor shalt thou deceive your children by pretending that you listen to every word. Rather, thou shalt encourage your children to tune in as much as they can and refrain from making them feel guilty when they tune out.

9. Thou shalt not place undue emphasis on peer groupings and the nuclear family within the life of your congregation. Rather, thou shalt teach your children to think of their congregation as the extended family of Jesus. Thou shalt do everything possible to help them meet, know and love members of this family. Thou shalt particularly encourage friendships between different age groups. Thou shalt let your small children know that it is O.K. to sit with various adult members of their extended family during the worship service.

10. Thou shalt countenance neither organisation nor attitude which makes if difficult for children to regularly worship with their congregation.

The EEL principle of ministry with children

Some adults who want to welcome children into worship and other aspects of their church life are simply not sure as to how to go about it. For instance many old people have the notion that modern children will not like them. Some childless adults have never felt at ease with children. Some young people feel that children will only like them if they speak and behave in an exaggerated manner. Some ministers feel ill equipped to communicate with children.

Congregations that are soon to welcome children into worship can do with some gentle coaching in the art of relating to children. One way of doing this is to share with them in print or in words simple formulas like the EEL principle.

E   Relating to children is *easier* than you think
    What children mostly want of you is to be yourself.

    Children will not mind if:
        you talk slowly or fast;
        you are fat or thin;
        you are formal or informal;
        you are mod or old fashioned.

    Children want you to like them and care about them:
        they want you to notice them;
        they want you to listen to them;
        they want you to talk with them;
        they want to know your name;
        they want to tell you theirs.

E   Relating to children is *expensive*
    Children need a lot from their true friends:
        they need time to share things;
        they need patience because they are often slow;
        they need forgiveness for they make many obvious mistakes.

Friendship with children is costly:
  children need to see their friend often;
  children need to have access to your home;
  children need to have access to your heart;
  children need to have access to your life.

L Relating to children is *life-giving*
Children are not mean:
  they will share their deepest thoughts
  they want to share their homes and their families;
  their greatest joy is to help their friends.

They try to give more than they get:
  they are expert at forgiving and forgetting
  they love wonderfully;
  they teach their friends everything they know;
  they will share their life force with those who love them;
  they give their beauty to their friends — this can be seen in
  the twinkle in the eyes of the friends of children.

Appendix II
For emergency use only

If you want to go to worship with children, and your church is making it hard for you — try a little subversion!

Copy this page and nail it to your church door — or send it to your congregation's decision-making council.

A bill of rights
for adults and children who wish to go to church together

For the purpose of this bill, the word 'children' includes all persons from birth to twelve years.

The following are the rights of adults and children who wish to attend the worship of their church together.

It is affirmed that they have the right to do so.

It is affirmed that children have the right to stay with their adult companion(s) for the duration of the entire worship service.

This right remains unaltered even in congregations that:

organise Sunday school or Junior Church at the same time as worship;

provide a nursery or creche or some other child minding facility;

have a crying room.

Further, it is affirmed that it is the right of a parent or parents or an adult friend who is acting with the parent(s) permission, to discourage the children in their care from using any of the provisions mentioned above.

It is affirmed that these persons have the right to expect their congregation to express welcome and show warmth to them before and after and in appropriate ways, during the worship service.

It is affirmed that it is the right of children to be greeted and farewelled with courtesy. Part of this greeting should include the provision of all appropriate books and papers necessary for participation in the worship service. This provision is to be automatic and not dependent on the child's ability to read.

In congregations where infants are baptised, it is affirmed that children and parents have the right to expect the congregation to honour the promises made in the baptismal service. This includes consistent, prayerful care for the children and their parents. It also includes continued practical acknowledgment that the children are valued members of the congregation.

In congregations were infant baptism is not practised, it is affirmed that the children have a right to share in the love of the congregation and to be constantly mentioned in the prayer of the congregation.

It is affirmed that the children who attend a church are in fact children of the entire congregation — not just children of their parents. Because this is the case, these children and their parents have the right to expect that, from time to time, members of the congregation will share in the nurturing of the children in formal and informal ways. Part of this includes the right of the child to receive pastoral care from the congregation's caregivers. It also includes the right of the child to visit the homes of the members of their church families and be welcome there.

These rights are based upon:
>the ministry of Jesus as revealed in his words and actions;
>all of the New Testament images of the church;
>the practice of the church universal throughout the centuries (excluding the last 30 years in a handful of denominations);
>the spiritual and psychological needs of children;
>the spiritual and fellowship needs of adults;
>the nature of the gospel and of the kingdom of God.

If you decide to use the *Bill of Rights* you will need to be well versed in what follows.

A Bill of Responsibilities
for persons who wish to go to church with children

For personal and private use. Copy this out and nail it on the inside of your wardrobe door — or wherever you will see it frequently.

Persons who accompany children to worship are responsible for preparing these children for the experience. This will include explanations at the child's level of the meaning and importance of the gathering; developing the children's ability to handle times of quiet and inactivity; modelling appropriate behaviour and preparing in advance strategies for coping with times of emergencies (when the service goes too long or a child cannot contain his/her restlessness).

Persons who accompany children to worship are responsible for making sure that during the service the children behave in an appropriate way. This means any noise the children might make be kept below the level of adult coughing and other accepted noises (street noises, etc.) which are regularly heard in the worship sanctuary.

In the event of a child creating excessive noise and/or disturbance, it is the responsibility of the person who accompanied that child to worship to take him/her out of the service until such time as the child calms down.

When the child is quietened, it is then that person's responsibility to take them back into the worship service again — even if that service is near to its conclusion.

When the person who accompanies the child is also the parent, it is that person's responsibility to give encouragement to the formation of relationships between the child and the adults of the church. As part of this responsibility, the parent should seek to foster close relationships between at least one or two adults and their child.

When the person who accompanies the child is not the parent, they should take care to introduce the child to other adults and take steps to see that the child is personally welcomed by at least some of the adults of the church.